✛ ✛ ✛

INTRODUCING CHRISTIANITY

✛ ✛ ✛

INTRODUCING CHRISTIANITY

BY

MICHAEL KEENE

Westminster John Knox Press
Louisville, Kentucky

Published in 1998 by
Westminster John Knox Press
Louisville, Kentucky

Copyright © 1998 Hunt & Thorpe

Text © 1998 Michael Keene

First published in Great Britain under the title
Introducing Christianity by
Hunt and Thorpe, New Alresford, Hants

The publishers are grateful to the following for permission to reproduce
photographs: AKG pp14, 28, 115C, 135; Bridgeman Art Library p7;
e.t. archive pp43, 64, 91, 94; Fortean Picture Library pp119, 123;
Stock Market p121

Designed by
THE BRIDGEWATER BOOK COMPANY

Printed in Hong Kong

98 99 00 01 02 03 04 05 06 07 – 10 9 8 7 6 5 4 3 2 1

Library of Congress Cataloging-in-Publication Data

Keene, Michael
    Introducing Christianity / Michael Keene. – 1st ed.
        p. cm.
        ISBN 0-664-25790-9
            1. Christianity. 2. Church history. 3. Christian sects.
    I. Title.
    BR121.2.K39   1998
    230–dc21   98-9950

CONTENTS

INTRODUCTION
THE CHRISTIAN FAITH

No other religion is so completely identified with the life and teachings of one man as Christianity. This religious faith centers its whole meaning around Jesus Christ, the founder of the faith and the Son of God. Its Holy Scriptures, the New Testament, revolve around the birth, the teachings, the actions, the death, and the resurrection of this one man. From his inspiration and example, Christians have found forgiveness for their own sins and the strength to serve God in the world.

The same inspiration also led to the founding of the Christian Church which, worldwide, now offers a spiritual home to some 1,500 million followers. But of course, over 2,000 years of history there have been countleess developments, arguments, splits and reconciliations, reformations and counter-reformations. Just as the modern world would be unrecognizable to the simple farmers and fishermen of Roman-occupied Palestine, so modern critics of the Church might claim that Christianity has moved a long way from the early community of faith.

This book offers a simple introduction to Christianity, examining some of the ways it has developed, and considering also the basic beliefs that have remained unchanged. In non-technical language it offers a breakdown of Christianity into eight chapters ranging from Jesus and the early Christian community to the major Churches, the Bible, religious ceremonies and Christian beliefs. There is also a full glossary which offers a definition of all the technical words used in the text. The book is enlivened and illustrated throughout with original photographs taken by the author's son, Alex Keene, who has collaborated with his father on all of his recent books.

LEFT: *Christianity is the most widespread of the world's religions.*

RIGHT: *For Christians the Cross is a reminder of the resurrection of Jesus which healed the relationship between God and humanity.*

FAR RIGHT: *The person and teachings of Jesus are the focus of the Christian religion.*

JESUS AND THE EARLY CHURCH

*"After he had been
baptized by John
the Baptist, Jesus heard a voice
from heaven telling him:
'You are my own dear Son.
I am pleased with you.'"*

MARK 1.11

1.1
WHO WAS JESUS?

The Romans, under Pompey, conquered Palestine and occupied the whole country. For the Jewish inhabitants this experience of captivity was a very familiar one and they longed for God to send them the much-awaited Messiah. Their Scriptures had been full of this mysterious figure who would deliver them from their enemies and set up God's Kingdom on earth. Most Jews were looking for a military leader although some expected a prophet in the tradition of Moses or a king like the much-loved David of old.

When Jesus appeared many people were convinced that their Messiah had come but Jesus was reluctant to apply the title to himself. He had no intention of leading a military uprising against the

Galatians 4.4

In his letter to the Christians in Galatia, Paul wrote:
"When the right time finally came, God sent his own Son. He came as the son of a human mother and lived under the Jewish Law, to redeem those who were under the Law, so that we might become God's sons and daughters."

Romans nor was he a typical Jewish prophet or king. His "kingdom" was spiritual and not political - the "Kingdom of God," which was to be set up in the hearts and minds of the people. After he left the earth, however, his followers lost no time in preaching that Jesus was the Messiah and it was this message that led

to the final break between Judaism and Christianity. The Jews, as a whole, rejected the claim while the Christians put it at the center of their mission. They even took the Greek word for Messiah, "Christos" - anointed by God - and turned it into a surname for Jesus.

Why were they so sure? The time that they had spent with Jesus convinced them that he was the Messiah since he announced the coming of God's Kingdom, as the Scriptures promised he would, fed large crowds miraculously, cast out demons, and forgave sins.

THE SON OF GOD AND THE SON OF MAN

Jesus was reluctant for people to call him the Messiah since he thought that the title could only confuse the people. The early Christians often called Jesus "the Son of God" although the title only crops up occasionally in the Gospels. It drew attention to the unique relationship that Jesus had with God, his Father. This relationship can be best expressed by that

which exists between a human father and his son. Jesus shocked his disciples by even calling God "Abba" [Daddy] - a term that indicated the closest possible relationship.

Jesus preferred to call himself "the Son of Man." It was a phrase that was familiar to his Jewish listeners from their Scriptures. More often than not, the Scriptures simply referred to "humankind" but they also spoke of a figure of great spiritual authority

Mark 1.11

*"After he had been baptized by John the Baptist, Jesus heard a voice from heaven telling him:
'You are my own dear Son.
I am pleased with you.'"*

who, at the end of time, would be given by God an everlasting kingdom to rule over.

Put these different titles together and we can form an idea of how Jesus saw himself - and how others saw him. As the Messiah he had come to offer spiritual deliverance to

THE NICENE CREED

A creed is a statement of belief. Perhaps the most important creed in the history of Christianity was the Nicene Creed, first used in Antioch in the late 5th century. It is used in the Eucharist of the Roman Catholic, Anglican, and Eastern Orthodox Churches. The Nicene Creed says this about Jesus: **"For us men and our salvation, he came down from heaven; by the power of the Holy Spirit he became incarnate of the Virgin Mary and was made man. For our sake he was crucified under Pontius Pilate, he suffered death and was buried. On the third day he rose again in accordance with the Scriptures..."**

the people from their sins. As God's Son he enjoyed a unique relationship with God, and yet, as the Son of Man, he identified totally with the human race. So Christians soon came to see in Jesus the unique person who was both fully God and fully human.

LEFT: *A modern sculpture of Christ tries to bring together what is known about him and what is believed by faith.*

IN THE GLOSSARY

Gospels ✢ John the Baptist
Kingdom of God ✢ Messiah
Moses ✢ Palestine ✢ Prophet
Son of God ✢ Son of Man

1.2

BEGINNINGS

We cannot construct a simple account of the life of Jesus from the Gospels nor can we discover much information from them about the early life of Jesus. Matthew [chapters 1 and 2] and Luke [1.1-2.21] describe the birth of Jesus and events that took place in the early months of his life. In addition Luke gives us an account of the visit of the 12 year-old Jesus to the Temple with his parents [2.41-52] but, except for these episodes, the Gospels are silent.

THE BIRTH OF JESUS

It was during the sixth century that monks began to calculate when Jesus might have been born. We now know that they were several years out in their calculations. Herod the Great died in 4 B.C.E. and he was clearly alive when Jesus was born [Matthew 2.1]. When he heard that Jesus, the king, had been born he tried to kill him by putting all male babies under the age of two to the sword in Jerusalem [Matthew 2.16] - an event that is remembered by some Churches each year on December 28th as Holy Innocents Day.

Christians have always believed that Jesus was born in Bethlehem. This fulfilled those Old Testament prophecies that the Messiah would be born in this small village, five miles south of Jerusalem. Bethlehem was also the birthplace of King

LEFT: A crib portraying the traditional picture of the birth of Jesus. In their accounts both Matthew and Luke stressed their belief that Jesus had come to earth to offer human beings forgiveness for their sins.

David. Both Matthew and Luke offer genealogies that trace the line of Jesus back to David but the names in their lists are different. Some scholars suggest that Jesus was actually born in Nazareth, his own home town in Galilee.

According to the Gospels the mother of Jesus was Mary, a teenager who was a virgin when she conceived him by the Holy Spirit. His father was Joseph, a carpenter from Bethlehem. Luke informs us that they had to travel to Bethlehem to satisfy a Roman ruling that everyone should travel to their home town to be counted in a census. When they made this difficult journey, with Mary heavily pregnant, there was no room for them in the village, so Jesus was born in a stable. His name, Jesus, meant "God saves."

Luke 1.32,33

According to Luke an angel appeared to Mary to tell her that she would bear Jesus. Concerning her child the angel said:
"He will be great and will be called the Son of the Most High God. The Lord God will make him a king, as his ancestor David was, and he will be the king of the descendants of Jacob [the Jews]; his kingdom will never end."

According to Luke the first to come to pay their respects to the child were poor shepherds to whom an angel had appeared. This established in the reader's mind those people who were to pay most respect to the teaching of Jesus throughout his ministry - the poor. Matthew, though, tells us of "Magi" [star-gazers, astrologers] from the East who brought the Christ-child the symbolic gifts of gold, frankincense, and myrrh. These served as reminders of Christ's kingship and his reception by the Gentiles.

FROM CHILDHOOD ONWARD

There are no other stories about the childhood of Jesus until he reached the age of 12 and accompanied his parents on their yearly trip to the Temple in Jerusalem. Left behind in the city by mistake, he was discovered by his parents discussing the finer points of the Torah, [Jewish Law] with the scribes and rabbis "listening to them and asking questions. All who heard him were amazed at his intelligent answers" [Luke 2.46,47]. When scolded by his parents he replied to them: "Why did you have to look for me? Didn't you know that I had to be in my Father's house?" His parents did not understand his answer. The story shows that Jesus had a strong sense of mission, even as a child, as well as a detailed knowledge of Jewish tradition and Scriptures. He also had a strong sense of the presence of God.

The New Testament then falls silent about Jesus. Instead, it describes the ministry of John the Baptist, a prophet sent by God who carried out a Jewish form of baptism in the Jordan River and began to speak of the coming of the Kingdom of God. Because the Jews were suffering under the pressure from the Romans Jewish expectations about a Messiah and God's Kingdom were very high at the time. By stirring them up John the Baptist was preparing the way for the coming of Jesus.

At the age of 30 Jesus appeared to be baptized by John [Matthew 3.13-17]. John was challenging people to repent of their sins and to be spiritually purified by immersion beneath the water. He did not feel that it was appropriate for Jesus to be baptized but Jesus insisted. Jesus probably

Mark 1.11

Mark's description of the aftermath to the baptism of Jesus:
"As soon as Jesus came up out of the water, he saw heaven opening and the Spirit coming down on him like a dove. And a voice came from heaven, 'You are my own dear Son. I am pleased with you.'"

saw it as a way to consecrate himself for his work ahead as the Messiah. Also, by being baptized, he was identifying himself with sinful men and women.

According to the Gospel writers Jesus followed his baptism by undertaking a 40-day fast in the wilderness [Matthew 4.1-11]. During this fast he was tempted by the Devil, Satan, to use his spiritual power for nonspiritual ends. He refused and emerged from the desert to begin his ministry.

IN THE GLOSSARY

Angel ✦ Baptism ✦ Bethlehem
David ✦ Gospels ✦ Herod the Great
Holy Spirit ✦ Jerusalem ✦ John the
Baptist ✦ Joseph ✦ Kingdom of God
Luke ✦ Mary ✦ Matthew ✦ Messiah
Nazareth ✦ New Testament
Old Testament ✦ Rabbi ✦ Satan
Temple ✦ Torah

1.3
THE TEACHINGS OF JESUS

The Gospels are not simply made up of the teachings of Jesus, much was added later by the early Church and the editors of the Gospels to suit their intended audiences. While the Gospel of Matthew, for instance, was written for Jewish readers, Luke had a largely Gentile audience in mind for his Gospel. The evidence suggests that Jesus was recognized as an outstanding teacher and was called "rabbi" [teacher]. Technically, though, he was not a rabbi since men who wanted to enter that honorable profession passed through an extensive period of training. In Jesus, the people simply saw a considerable gift for teaching combined with a distinctive emphasis in all that he said.

JESUS, THE TEACHER

At the beginning of his ministry Jesus taught in the Jewish places of worship [synagogues] but when that was no longer possible he moved into the open air. The people brought their questions about the Jewish Law [the Torah] to him and in reply he taught them about such matters as paying taxes to the Romans [Mark 12.13-17], adultery [John 7.53-8.11], marriage and divorce [Mark 10.1-12]. By bringing their questions about the Torah to Jesus the people were treating him as a rabbi and this was probably one of the ways in which he most annoyed the Jewish authorities.

Along with other spiritual teachers of the day Jesus taught mainly in parables - human stories that were intended to have a spiritual meaning. The Jewish holy books were full of such stories - called "mishnah." With one exception - the parable of the sower in Mark 4.1-20 -

Matthew 5.3

In the Beatitudes Jesus said:
*"Happy are those who know that
they are spiritually poor;
the Kingdom of God belongs to them."*

LEFT: The picture of Jesus preaching to his disciples is from one of the early Bibles that was illuminated [decorated] by monks.

Jesus left his stories open so that his listeners could draw their own conclusions from them.

Jesus also used other ways of teaching:

❖ He lodged a short, memorable saying in the minds of his listeners. After disagreeing with the Pharisees over how his disciples should behave on the Sabbath Day he told them: "The Son of Man is Lord of the Sabbath" [Luke 6.5]. On another occasion he said that: "One blind man cannot lead another one; if he does, both will fall into a ditch" [Luke 6.39]. These short sayings made it easy for his listeners to remember what he had said.

❖ He used vivid and familiar images. We can see this in the so-called Sermon on the Mount [Matthew 5-7] which is, in

Matthew 22.34-40

The whole teaching of Jesus can be summed up by this extract: "'Teacher,' he asked, 'which is the greatest commandment in the Law?' Jesus answered, 'Love the Lord your God with all your heart, with all your soul, and with all your mind. This is the greatest and most important commandment. The second most important commandment is like it: Love your neighbor as you love yourself. The whole Law and the teachings of the prophets depend on these two commandments.'"

fact, a collection of the teachings of Jesus brought together by Matthew. Among the images he used were light, salt, birds, flowers, and a city set on a hill. In John's Gospel, Jesus spoke of himself as "the true vine," "the good shepherd," "bread," and "life-giving water" among other things.

✢   He used exaggeration. Jesus often exaggerated deliberately to emphasize the point that he wanted to make. In Matthew 5.29 and 30 Jesus spoke of cutting off any part of the body that causes offense. After a rich man was put off from becoming a disciple Jesus told his disciples that it was easier for a camel to go through the eye of a needle than for a rich man to enter God's Kingdom [Matthew 19. 23].

THE MESSAGE

What was Jesus trying to say through his parables, sayings, images, and exaggerations? His whole teaching was concerned with one message - that God's Kingdom had come. Jesus himself had ushered in that Kingdom and he was now concerned to tell the people how they could belong to it. Mark summed this up beautifully at the beginning of his Gospel:

"The right time has come and the Kingdom of God is near! Turn away from your sins and believe the Good News" [Mark 1.15].

His Jewish listeners would have understood what Jesus was saying. For centuries their ancestors had been waiting for the coming of God's Messiah and here was Jesus announcing that their time of

waiting was over. Yet there was a very real sting in the tail. Jesus had not come to call the religious and the self-righteous into his kingdom, he had come for those on the very edge of society. Little wonder, then, that his message was welcomed by the tax-collectors, prostitutes, and demon-possessed. It was for them, more than others, that God's time had come.

IN THE GLOSSARY

Beatitudes ✢ Disciple ✢ Gentile
Gospel ✢ John ✢ Kingdom of God
Luke ✢ Matthew ✢ Messiah
Mishnah ✢ Parable
Pharisees ✢ Rabbi ✢ Sabbath Day
Sermon on the Mount
Synagogue ✢ Torah

1.4
THE MIRACLES
OF JESUS

In the synagogue in Nazareth, Jesus read a passage from the prophet Isaiah which said the Messiah [Christ] would bring "good news to the poor... liberty to the captives... recovery of sight to the blind... freedom to the oppressed..." [Luke 4.18]. The miracles Jesus performed were part of this message. They were also one of the main causes for the opposition that he encountered from the authorities.

WHOSE POWER?

While the people at the time seem to have accepted that Jesus performed miracles, there was great discussion about the source of his power and authority. The Jews believed that there were "good" and "false" prophets and that Jesus fitted firmly in the latter group. That is why we find the scribes insisting that Jesus performed miracles by the power of Satan and not God [Mark 3.22-26]. At the end of the first century Josephus, a Jewish historian, confirmed that Jesus had extraordinary powers as "a doer of wonderful deeds and a teacher of those who receive the truth gladly." He did not, however, come to any firm conclusion about the source of Jesus' power.

MIRACLES?

The most striking feature of the life of Jesus presented by all four Gospels is the emphasis that each of them places on his miracles. We frequently encounter a Jesus with the power to cast out devils, cure illness, and curb the unruly elements of nature with a single word. There are four reasons why these miracles played such an important role in the ministry of Jesus as the Gospels present it:

a. JESUS WAS DEEPLY MOVED BY THE NEEDS OF THE PEOPLE. He fed 5,000 men, women, and children miraculously from loaves and fish because "his heart was filled with pity for them, because they were like sheep without a shepherd" [Mark 6.34]. He healed two blind men who cried out to him for help [Matthew 9.27-31], and brought his friend Lazarus back to life

John 6.27

In his Gospel John provides us with a comment by Jesus on the true meaning of the feeding of a large crowd:
"I am telling you the truth: you are looking for me because you ate the bread and had all you wanted, not because you understand my miracles. Do not work for food that goes bad; instead, work for the food that lasts for eternal life. This is the food which the Son of Man will give you, because God, the Father, has put his mark of approval on him."

BELOW: The miracles of Jesus, as the one shown in this stained-glass window, were an important part of the message of Jesus.

LEFT: *Jesus' miracle of the loaves and fishes is commemorated in this modern sculpture. This miracle was greatly loved by the early Christians since it pointed toward the Eucharist.*

because "his heart was touched and he was deeply moved" [John 11.33].

b. HE RESPONDED TO THE FAITH THAT THE PEOPLE SHOWED IN HIM. The Roman centurion expressed his faith that Jesus did not even need to go to his house to cure his servant: "Just give the order and my servant will get well" [Matthew 8.8]. A woman who had been hemorrhaging for 12 years believed that she simply needed to touch the hem of Jesus' cloak in order to be healed [Luke 8. 43-48].

c. HE PERFORMED MIRACLES SO THAT FAITH WOULD BE BORN IN THOSE HE DELIVERED. Jesus was sound asleep in the back of the fishing boat that belonged to James and John, with his head on a cushion, when the disciples grew alarmed during a raging storm on the Sea of Galilee. Jesus awoke and quietened the storm with a single command - "Be still" - before saying to his disciples "Have you still no faith?" [Mark 4.39].

d. HE PERFORMED MIRACLES TO SHOW THE PEOPLE THAT THE KINGDOM OF GOD HAD COME. When John the Baptist was in prison he sent messengers to Jesus to find out whether he really was the Messiah. Jesus replied by telling the messengers to remind John of the miracles that Jesus was performing. They were the final proof that the rule of God on earth had begun. Although Jesus performed his miracles quietly and compassionately they are presented in the Gospels as signs of the Kingdom of God. The miracles also had a symbolic meaning for the early Christians.

IN THE GLOSSARY

Christ ✣ Disciple ✣ Gospels
Holy Communion ✣ John
John the Baptist ✣ Kingdom of God
Luke ✣ Messiah ✣ Nazareth
Prophet ✣ Satan ✣ Scribes
Synagogue

For example, the feeding of the 5,000 clearly carried two additional meanings:

✣ For Luke, in his account of the event, it was not just physical bread that he was talking about when he said "They all ate and had enough…" [Luke 9.17]. The people came to Jesus out of spiritual hunger and he fed them. Bread often symbolized life-giving sustenance, while, in John, Jesus offered himself up as "the Bread of Life."

✣ The miracle is the only one found in all four Gospels. If, as seems very likely, the two accounts of the feeding of the 4,000 refer to the same event as well, then this miracle is recorded six times. There must be a reason for this. Probably the early Christians saw a close link between this miracle and the fellowship meal that later was to become Holy Communion. As in that service so here Jesus was really feeding the crowd on himself.

1.5
CRUCIFIXION

Jesus knew he had aroused bitter opposition, especially from religious leaders. He also knew that matters would come to a head if he visited Jerusalem, the city that stood at the heart of the Jewish faith. To go there during the Jewish festival of Passover was an added provocation. But Jesus cared deeply about Jerusalem: "Jerusalem! Jerusalem! You kill the prophets, you stone the messengers God has sent you! How many times have I wanted to put my arms round your people, just as a hen gathers her chicks under her wings, but you would not let me!" [Luke 13.34]. What happened to Jesus in Jerusalem, during the last few days of his life, is crucial to understanding his whole ministry.

TOWARD THE END

On three separate occasions Jesus tried to warn his disciples of what lay ahead. They did not understand him and even those disciples closest to Jesus [Peter, James, and John] could not come to terms with a suffering and dying Messiah. When he left the earth, however, his undeserved suffering and death became the very heart of the early Church's message.

Having entered the city of Jerusalem on a donkey, Jesus was given a welcome by the crowd, which showed that they recognized him to be a king [Mark 11.1-11]. A few days later he withdrew with his disciples to eat a Passover meal [Mark 14.12-26]. At this he used bread and wine to teach his disciples about the meaning of his death and this became the basis of the Holy Communion service. At the same time Judas Iscariot was discovered to be the disciple who would betray Jesus for 30 pieces of silver.

Jesus then took three of his disciples with him to the Garden of Gethsemane on the slopes of the Mount of Olives.

1 Corinthians 11.23-25

These are the words of Paul describing the last meal that Jesus shared with his disciples:

"…the Lord Jesus, on the night he was betrayed, took a piece of bread, gave thanks to God, broke it, and said, 'This is my body, which is for you. Do this in memory of me.' In the same way, after the supper he took the cup and said, 'This cup is God's new covenant, sealed with my blood. Whenever you drink it, do so in memory of me.'"

There he prayed intensely that God would take the cup of suffering from him, "yet not what I want but what you want"

[Mark 14.36]. Three times Jesus looked to his disciples for support but each time they had fallen asleep, bringing the comment by Jesus "The spirit is willing but the flesh is weak" [Mark 14.38]. Eventually Jesus accepted what lay ahead of him as a crowd, led by Judas, approached with swords and clubs. Jesus was led away to be questioned by the chief priests, elders, and scribes.

DEATH

The Gospels tell us of the two "trials" of Jesus:

1. THE APPEARANCE BEFORE THE HIGH PRIEST, CAIAPHAS, and members of the Sanhedrin. Caiaphas asked Jesus several questions to establish whether he was a blasphemer. One concerned the claim that he was the Son of God. Jesus answered him: "So you say. But I tell all of you: from this time on you will see the Son of Man sitting on the right hand of the Almighty and coming on the clouds of heaven"

[Matthew 26.64]. Caiaphas said that this was blasphemy and they took Jesus to Pontius Pilate, the Roman procurator.

2. THE APPEARANCE BEFORE PILATE. Three charges were laid against Jesus: that he had misled the people; that he had encouraged the people not to pay their taxes to Rome; and that he had claimed to be king. To Pilate's leading question, "Are you the King of the Jews?" Jesus simply replied, "So you say." For this Jesus was condemned to death and taken to a hill named Golgotha and nailed to a cross. The accusation - "This is Jesus, the King of the Jews" - was pinned above him and two criminals were put to death on either side of him. The authorities, the crowd, and even the criminals mocked him for being able to save others when he could not save himself.

Jesus hung there for six hours, according

ABOVE: *This Station of the Cross shows the Crucifixion of Jesus. The death of Jesus on the cross is the most powerful, and important, symbol in the Christian faith.*

Romans 5.8,9

Paul wrote this about the death of Jesus: *"God has shown us how much he loves us - it was while we were still sinners that Christ died for us! By his blood we are now put right with God; how much more, then, will we be saved by him from God's anger."*

to the Gospels, before crying out in Aramaic "Eli, Eli, lama sabachthani" meaning, "My God, my God, why did you abandon me?" [Matthew 27.46]. Jesus then died. This event is thought to have happened in 29 or 30 C.E. A wealthy follower of Jesus, Joseph of Arimathea, asked Pontius Pilate for the body of Jesus, wrapped it in a linen shroud, and placed it in the tomb that he had prepared for himself. A guard was placed at the door to make sure that no followers of Jesus stole the body.

IN THE GLOSSARY

Aramaic ✤ Blasphemy ✤ Caiaphas
Disciple ✤ Gethsemane ✤ Golgotha
Gospel ✤ High Priest
Holy Communion ✤ James
Jerusalem ✤ John ✤ Judas Iscariot
Messiah ✤ Passover ✤ Paul
Peter ✤ Pontius Pilate

1.6
RESURRECTION

According to the New Testament, Jesus rose from the dead on the third day after his crucifixion, and belief in the resurrection stands at the very heart of the Christian faith. Without it, as Paul reminded his readers, that faith would be little more than a tragic delusion. The early Church believed that Jesus was living through the Holy Spirit in the Christian community, which was born on the Day of Pentecost.

THE GOSPELS AND THE RESURRECTION

Each of the four Gospels reports that the tomb that held the body of Jesus was empty. They do not, however, all tell the same story. Perhaps this is hardly surprising since the resurrection of Jesus seems to have taken his followers totally by surprise. As with all the material in the Gospels, the Evangelists selected and shaped their accounts to emphasize their own particular view about Jesus.

The Gospels do not explain what happened to the body of Jesus. Mark, for instance, leaves us with an empty tomb without relating any of the later appearances of Jesus - 16.9-20 does not belong to the original Gospel. It is the other Gospel writers who are interested in the "appearances" although the exact way in which these happened is open to great doubt. There was certainly a very real change in the appearance of Jesus after his resurrection - it took people longer to recognize him [Luke 24.13-35; John 20.14]; he walked through locked doors [John 20.19-23]; and he appeared and disappeared at will [Luke 24.36]. According to the New Testament Jesus appeared to

+ Mary Magdalene and "the other Mary" [Matthew 28.1-10]
+ Mary Magdalene, Salome, and Mary, the mother of James [Mark 16.1-8]
+ two disciples walking from Jerusalem to Emmaus [Luke 24.13-35]
+ the 11 disciples [Mark 16.14; Luke 24.36-49]
+ five hundred of his followers [1 Corinthians 15.6].
+ James [1 Corinthians 15.7].
+ all of the Apostles [1 Corinthians 15.7].

THE MEANING OF THE RESURRECTION

The importance of the resurrection of Jesus lies in its meaning. According to the New Testament provided the proof that Jesus was who he claimed to be - God's Messiah. Preaching to a Jewish audience on the Day of Pentecost Peter declared: "God has raised this very Jesus from death, and we are all witnesses to this fact. He has been raised to the right-hand side of God, his Father, and has received from him the Holy Spirit, as he had promised… All of the people of Israel, then, are to

Matthew 28.19,20

The last recorded words of Jesus in Matthew's Gospel:
"Go, then, to all peoples everywhere and make them my disciples: baptize them in the name of the Father, the Son, and the Holy Spirit, and teach them to obey everything I have commanded you. And I will be with you always, to the end of the age."

know for sure that this Jesus, whom you crucified, is the one that God has made the Lord and Messiah" [Acts 2.32,33,36].

The link in Peter's sermon between the resurrection of Jesus and the giving of the Holy Spirit is very important. Through his being brought back from the dead by God,

⊹ ⊹ ⊹

THE NICENE CREED

⊹ ⊹ ⊹

The Nicene Creed links the resurrection of Jesus with his return from heaven at the "Second Coming":

On the third day he rose again in accordance with the Scriptures; he ascended into heaven and is seated on the right hand of the Father.

He will come again in glory to judge the living and the dead, and his kingdom will have no end."

RIGHT: After his resurrection, Jesus appeared to two of his disciples on the road from Jerusalem to Emmaus.

Jesus has released a new kind of power on humankind - that of the Holy Spirit. Jesus had promised that this would happen. The Spirit, he told his disciples, would lead them all into truth and remind them of what they had learned from Jesus [John 16.13].

The resurrection of Jesus from the dead was also a guarantee that, at the end of time, all those who believed in him would rise from the dead. Paul makes much of this when writing to the Christians in Corinth. He told them that the resurrection of Jesus was established beyond any doubt, and because of this their own future resurrection from the dead was also guaranteed.

THE ASCENSION INTO HEAVEN

Luke's Gospel ends and the Acts of the Apostles begins with the ascension of Jesus into heaven. Both of these books were written by the same person and were probably originally intended to be two parts of one work. The ascension provides a very neat end to the life of Jesus. Needless to say, though, the idea of Jesus going upward into heaven causes a great problem to modern Christians. Many Churches try to reinterpret the event when they celebrate Ascension Day, in May, each year.

IN THE GLOSSARY

Acts of the Apostles ⊹ Apostle
Day of Pentecost ⊹ Disciple
Gospel ⊹ Holy Spirit ⊹ James
Mark ⊹ Messiah ⊹ New Testament
Nicene Creed ⊹ Paul ⊹ Peter

1.7

THE EARLY CHRISTIAN COMMUNITY

Luke ends his Gospel by describing Jesus leading his disciples out to the village of Bethany where he blessed them before being taken up into heaven. The disciples returned, with great joy, to Jerusalem where they "spent all their time in the Temple giving thanks to God" [24.52]. He opens the second part of his account, the Acts of the Apostles, with the ascension of Jesus into heaven [until "a cloud hid him from their sight"] with two men dressed in white [angels] telling them: "This Jesus, who was taken from you into heaven, will come back in the same way that you saw him go into heaven" [1.11].

THE DAY OF PENTECOST

The Jewish festival of Passover [Pesach], during which Jesus died, was followed 50 days later by the festival of Pentecost [the Feast of Weeks] or Shavuot. In Roman times this harvest festival brought Jews from all over the Empire to Jerusalem to celebrate the giving of the precious Law [the Torah] to Moses on Mount Sinai. Luke described what happened at this particular Pentecost, although, like other writers in the New Testament, he was not recording "history" in our sense of that word. He was writing, as an evangelist, to persuade others to believe in Jesus. We do not know precisely what happened in Jerusalem on this day but Luke provides us with the only description we have of the birth of the Christian Church.

For several weeks the disciples had huddled together in the city waiting for the spiritual power that Jesus had promised.

They remembered his words: "When the Holy Spirit comes upon you, you will be filled with power and you will be witnesses for me in Jerusalem, in all Judea and Samaria and to the ends of the earth" [Acts 1.8]. In the supernatural event that followed Luke tells us that the coming of God's Spirit was like a strong driving wind which filled the house in which the

Acts 2.38

On the Day of Pentecost the people were greatly challenged by Peter's message and wondered what they should do.
He told them:
"Each one of you must turn away from your sins and be baptized in the name of Jesus Christ, so that your sins will be forgiven; and you will receive God's gift, the Holy Spirit."

followers of Christ were gathered. The wind symbolized the uncontrollable and all-powerful Spirit of God; the flames of fire resting on each believer symbolized the Spirit's purifying qualities.

PETER

In the sermon that day, Peter, the leader of the disciples, made three points that formed the basis of the early Church's preaching. He told the people that:

✤ Jesus was the Messiah who had been crucified and brought back to life by God [Acts 2.36].

✤ Jesus had been given the highest place in heaven [Acts 2.33,34].

✤ All those who repent of their sins and believe in the Gospel will be forgiven by God [Acts 2.38].

On the first day alone, according to the Acts, more than 3,000 people who heard this message became believers. The

Christian Church was born and, very soon, would spread throughout the Roman Empire. Peter was the rock on which the early Church was built. He undertook preaching tours but, as a Jew, seemed unable to accept that non-Jews [Gentiles] should be welcomed into the Church as equal partners. He was superseded by Paul who, before his conversion, had ruthlessly persecuted the Christians. He became a tireless letter-writer and traveler in the cause of the Gospel - as you will discover in section 1.8. He made three missionary journeys to the limits of the Roman Empire and founded many churches.

During these years the Christians worshiped either in Jewish synagogues or, later, in each other's homes. It was to be several centuries before churches, as places of worship, were built. During this time there were many periods of persecution but the Church survived. Soon a quite elaborate system of organization grew up, with bishops appointed to look after the groups of Christians that were springing up everywhere. The situation of the Christian Church in the Roman Empire changed dramatically when Constantine [274-337] became the Emperor. Constantine, according to legend, was converted to Christianity on the eve of the battle of Milvian Bridge, in 312 C.E., when he saw a vision of a flaming cross with the words, in Greek: "In this sign conquer." He went out to gain a most improbable victory and Christianity became the official religion of the Roman Empire.

RIGHT: The Apostle Peter. Jesus named Peter "the rock" and entrusted him with the "keys of the Kingdom of Heaven."

IN THE GLOSSARY

Acts of the Apostles ✣ Bishop
Constantine ✣ Disciple
Feast of Weeks ✣ Gentiles ✣ Gospel
Holy Spirit ✣ Jerusalem ✣ Luke
Messiah ✣ Moses ✣ New Testament
Passover ✣ Paul ✣ Pentecost
Peter ✣ Shavuot ✣ Synagogue
Temple ✣ Torah

1.8
PAUL

The first Christian martyr was Stephen who was appointed a deacon by the early Church to look after the collection of charity for widows in the Christian community. Soon afterward some Jews traveled to Jerusalem from Cyrene and Alexandria and accused Stephen of preaching against the Law of Moses [the Torah]. Stephen was taken in front of the High Priest and the Jewish Council [the Sanhedrin] to answer the charge. Stephen infuriated the Jewish leaders in his long speech to them and they arrested him, hounded him out of the city, and stoned him to death [Acts 6.8 - 7.60]. Today, some Churches celebrate the martyrdom of Stephen on December 26th.

SAUL OF TARSUS

At the time that Stephen was being put to death, Saul of Tarsus was causing havoc among the early Christians. Saul was a Pharisaic Jew, a strict observer of the Jewish law, a student of the great Jewish rabbi Gamaliel, and a Roman citizen.

Acts 26.17,18

In this, one of three descriptions of his conversion experience, Paul describes the work that Jesus gave him to do:

"I will rescue you from the people of Israel and from the Gentiles to whom I send you. You are to open their eyes and turn them from the darkness to light and from the power of Satan to God, so that through their faith in me they will have their sins forgiven and receive their place among God's chosen people."

ABOVE: *Paul preaching. Paul has been the dominant personality and thinker in two millennia of Christian history.*

The High Priest in Jerusalem granted him permission to travel to Damascus, round up many of the Christians, and bring them back to the city. It was on this journey to Damascus that Saul saw a light from heaven that was stronger than the sun and heard the voice of Jesus asking why he, Saul, was persecuting the Church. After a short time Saul was cured of the blindness that had been brought on by the experience, and he was received into the Church.

THE LEGACY OF PAUL

The enormous legacy that Paul bequeathed to the Christian Church has been felt in three very important ways:
1. AS A MISSIONARY. In around 45 C.E. Paul set out with another disciple, Barnabas, to undertake his first journey as a Christian missionary.

He made two later journeys around the Mediterranean world before returning to

Jerusalem in 58 C.E. Prior to this, though, he had taken part, in 51 C.E., in the Council of Jerusalem at which the early Church leaders debated the issue that was troubling the young Christian community more than any other at the time - should non-Jews [Gentiles] who became Christians follow a Jewish way of life. At that time, remember, most of the Christians were also Jews.

2 Corinthians 11.24-26

In one of his letters Paul wrote this vivid description of his own missionary travels:

"Five times I was given the thirty-nine lashes by the Jews; three times I was whipped by the Romans; and once I was stoned. I have been in three shipwrecks, and once I spent twenty-four hours in the water. In my many travels I have been in danger from fellow-Jews and Gentiles; there have been dangers in the cities, dangers in the wilds, dangers on the high seas, and dangers from false friends."

The outcome of the Council was to open up the Church to Gentiles without expecting them to live as Jews.

2. AS A CHURCH PLANTER. The Christian Church grew very quickly in Paul's time and he often established a new church after he had visited and preached in an area. Because most of the new converts came from a pagan background, their whole lifestyle needed to change before they could play an active part in the Christian Church.

3. AS A LETTER-WRITER. Paul wrote many letters [called "epistles"] to churches and individual Christians, and many of these are preserved in the New Testament - although not all of those that bear his name came from his pen.

Some of these letters are long and complex, such as Romans and 1 Corinthians - while others, such as Philemon and Titus, are brief. These letters were saved and circulated among all the churches in the area.

ABOVE: *Paul at first opposed the followers of Jesus, but became a Christian after a vision, and then worked hard to spread the Christian faith.*

IN THE GLOSSARY

Acts of the Apostles
Council of Jerusalem ✠ Deacon
Epistle ✠ High Priest ✠ Jerusalem
Martyr ✠ Moses ✠ New Testament
✠ Rabbi ✠ Sanhedrin ✠ Satan
Stephen ✠ Torah

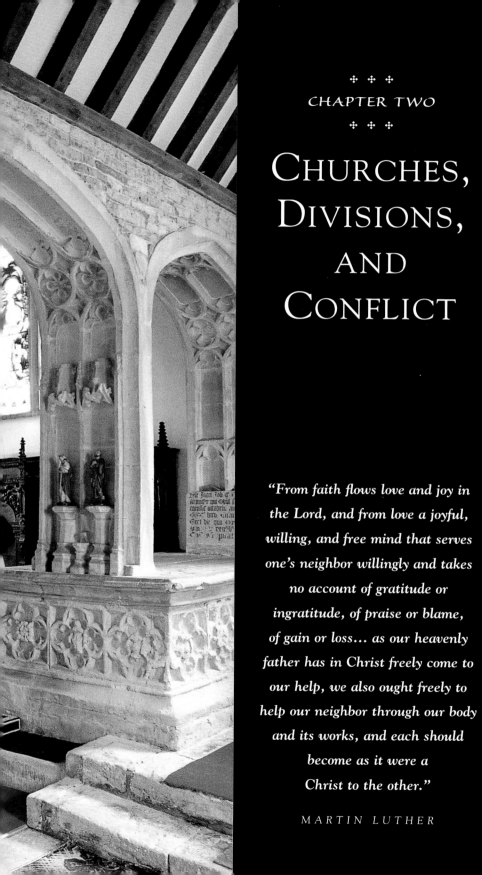

CHAPTER TWO

CHURCHES, DIVISIONS, AND CONFLICT

"From faith flows love and joy in the Lord, and from love a joyful, willing, and free mind that serves one's neighbor willingly and takes no account of gratitude or ingratitude, of praise or blame, of gain or loss… as our heavenly father has in Christ freely come to our help, we also ought freely to help our neighbor through our body and its works, and each should become as it were a Christ to the other."

MARTIN LUTHER

2.1
A DIVIDED CHURCH

Late in the third century C.E. the Roman Empire had been divided into an eastern and western section. In the fourth century C.E. Constantine, the Roman Emperor, established a second imperial seat in the East, in Constantinople. After the sack of Rome by the Goths in 410, Constantinople was looked upon as a "second Rome" and this had a profound effect upon the Church. The two parts of the Christian world grew apart, divided by language [Latin in the West and Greek in the East], culture, and religious differences.

A Council of Bishops, meeting at Chalcedon in 451, adopted a resolution that many Eastern bishops could not accept. As a result the Church began to show the first signs of later disintegration with the formation of the Eastern Oriental Church. It was not until 1054, however, that the split between East and West became final with the formation of the Eastern Orthodox [right belief] Church. The Orthodox Church broke away from the Roman Catholic Church over three main areas of disagreement:

+ The claim of the Pope in Rome to have supreme authority over the whole Church.
+ The desire of Rome to be acknowledged as the center of the Christian world.
+ A change by Rome in the wording of the Nicene Creed, which the Orthodox Churches considered to be inviolable.

So Christendom broke into two parts. The Orthodox Church was formed and the breach between it and the Roman Catholic Church has never been healed. After centuries of hostility and silence, these two Churches held an historic meeting in 1964 and have since begun talks with each other.

THE REFORMATION

In the centuries that followed the split between the Roman Catholic and Orthodox Churches dissatisfaction began to build up within the Roman Catholic Church. Matters came to a head in 1517 when Martin Luther, an obscure Catholic monk, nailed a list of 95 theses [grievances] to the door of his church in Wittenburg in Germany.

In them Luther argued that a Christian did not need to buy salvation through purchasing indulgences - as the Church taught. Instead, he argued, the Bible and not the Pope is the supreme authority in the Church, and the Bible

RIGHT: Martin Luther's protest against the teachings of the Catholic Church led to the creation of the Lutheran Church.

Martin Luther
A Treatise on Christian Liberty

"From faith flows love and joy in the Lord, and from love a joyful, willing, and free mind that serves one's neighbor willingly and takes no account of gratitude or ingratitude, of praise or blame, of gain or loss… as our heavenly father has in Christ freely come to our help, we also ought freely to help our neighbor through our body and its works, and each should become as it were a Christ to the other."

LEFT: *A long view of a Roman Catholic Church. This Church traces its roots back to the origins of Christianity although the Orthodox Church also claims to have the same roots.*

John 17.11

" *I pray for them. I do not pray for the world but for those you gave me, for they belong to you. All I have is yours and all you have is mine; and my glory is shown through them. And now I am coming to you; I am no longer in the world, but they are in the world. Holy Father! Keep them safe by the power of your name, the name that you gave me, so that they may be one as you and I are one.*"

teaches that any person can approach God directly for forgiveness without the need to go through a priest.

Luther's protest led to the birth of the "Protestant" movement and a further splintering of the Church. Luther was excommunicated [excluded from participating in Communion] but Churches based on his teaching were established.

In England, King Henry VIII fell out with the Pope over the Church's refusal to grant him a divorce. He declared himself to be the Head and Protector of the Church in England and its Supreme Governor.

The Church of England grew up under Elizabeth I and became the "established" [official] Church in the country. Churches in other parts of the world that grew out of the Church of England were called "Anglican."

THE NONCONFORMISTS

Before very long the Church of England itself was to splinter and break up. The new Churches were called "Nonconformist" because they did not "conform" to the teachings of the Church of England. They were also called "Free Churches" for the same reason. Among these Churches were the following:

IN THE GLOSSARY

Anglican ✢ Baptist Church ✢ Bible
Bishop ✢ Church of England
Constantine ✢ Excommunication
Free Churches ✢ House-Church
Movement ✢ Indulgence ✢ Methodist
Church ✢ Monk ✢ Nicene Creed
Nonconformist ✢ Pope ✢ Priest
Protestant Church ✢ Quakers
Reformation ✢ Roman Catholic Church
Salvation Army

✢ The Baptist Church, formed in the 17th century, which was largely based on the belief that only adult believers, and not children, could be baptized.

✢ The Quakers, formed by George Fox in the 17th century, with a simple, and largely silent, form of worship.

✢ The Methodist Church, established in the 18th century based on the teachings of John Wesley, who was a priest in the Church of England.

✢ The Salvation Army, which sprang out of Methodism in 1865.

Nonconformist Churches are still a part of the Christian scene, and others are coming into existence. In the 1970s the House-Church Movement was formed and it now has 20,000 members in Britain alone. Today, there are more than 20,000 different Churches - a far cry from the vision of their founder who prayed that all of his followers might be one.

2.2
THE ROMAN CATHOLIC CHURCH

The Roman Catholic Church, the largest of the denominations, includes 60% of all Christian believers. Although the Catholic Church is worldwide, it is strongest in North and South America and Europe. There is considerable debate over whether Peter became the first Bishop of Rome. By the fifth century C.E. the Bishop of Rome was claiming authority over the whole Christian community - a claim disputed in such places as Alexandria and Constantinople. This claim led to the final break between the Western and Eastern Churches and the power of the Pope ["papa" - daddy] was confined to the Western Churches.

Why "Roman" Catholic? There are two reasons why Catholics are called "Roman" Catholics:

1. THE NAME RECOGNIZES THE LEADERSHIP OF THE BISHOP OF ROME IN THE CHURCH. Catholics believe that the Pope's authority can be traced all the

Matthew 16. 17,18

The words spoken by Jesus to Peter provide the basis for the supreme authority of the Pope in the Roman Catholic Church:

"This truth did not come to you [Peter] from any human being, but it was given to you directly by my Father in heaven. And so I tell you, Peter; you are a rock, and on this rock foundation I will build my Church, and not even death will be able to overcome it."

way back to Peter who was appointed by Jesus to be the leader of the early Christians - and the first Bishop of Rome. The powers that Jesus gave to Peter are believed to have been transferred to each Papal successor by "the laying on of hands." This authority then allows each Pope to speak, from time to time, "ex cathedra" [from the throne], and when he does so each new teaching is incorporated into the official teaching of the Roman Catholic Church. This happened as recently as 1950 when Pope Pius XII declared that Mary, the mother of Jesus, did not die but was taken up bodily into heaven - a belief called "the Bodily Assumption of the Virgin Mary."

2. THE CHURCH IS "CATHOLIC" BECAUSE IT IS UNIVERSAL. Catholics see themselves belonging to the one, true Church with Christians in other Churches being "separated brethren."

CATHOLIC BELIEFS AND PRACTICE
Roman Catholics believe that all of their beliefs [dogma] are rooted in the teachings of Jesus and his Apostles together with the later traditions of the Church. The teaching authority of the Church, known as the "magisterium," resides in the collective ministry of all the bishops of the Church when they are gathered together into Ecumenical Councils. Many such Councils were held in the early centuries of the Church but, since the Reformation, there have been just three:

✢ the Council of Trent [1545-63].
✢ Vatican I [1870]
✢ Vatican II [1962-65].

Such Councils cannot change the teachings of the Church since these are fixed but they can change such matters as worship and the relationship of the Catholic Church with other religions. So Vatican II, for instance, determined that the Mass, the central act of Catholic worship, should be said in the language of the people and not the traditional Latin.

Among the most important beliefs of the Roman Catholic Church are the following: **a.** THE CENTRALITY OF THE MASS. This service, held daily in all Roman Catholic churches, reenacts the sacrifice of Jesus on the cross.

During the service the bread and wine become the actual body and blood of Jesus as Jesus promised they would. This belief in the transformation of bread and wine into the body and blood of Jesus, called "transubstantiation," is one of the clearest

Mark 14.22-24

"While they were eating, Jesus took a piece of bread, gave a prayer of thanks, broke it, and gave to his disciples. 'Take it,' he said, 'this is my body.' Then he took a cup, gave thanks to God, and handed it to them; and they all drank from it. Jesus said, 'This is my blood which is poured out for many, my blood which seals God's covenant.'"

differences between Roman Catholics and Protestants and a major point of disagreement that led to the Reformation. **b.** THE IMPORTANCE OF THE SAINTS AND THE VIRGIN MARY. The Virgin Mary, the mother of Jesus, is the focus of devotion for all Roman Catholics - as she is for members of the Orthodox Churches and many Anglicans. Many Catholics in the United States now speak of Mary being "co-redeemer" with Jesus. **c.** HEAVEN AND PURGATORY. Catholics

ABOVE: *The Mass being celebrated in a Roman Catholic church. This service, which reenacts the sacrifice of Christ on the cross, is at the center of all Catholic worship.*

share their belief in the existence of heaven with many other Christians but their belief in purgatory, an intermediate state designed to prepare souls for heaven, is a specifically Roman Catholic belief.

IN THE GLOSSARY

Anglican Church ✢ Apostle
Bishop ✢ Bishop of Rome
Magisterium ✢ Mary
Mass ✢ Orthodox Church
Peter ✢ Pope ✢ Protestant
Purgatory ✢ Reformation
Roman Catholic Church ✢ Saint
Transubstantiation

2.3
THE ORTHODOX CHURCH

Within a few centuries after the death of Jesus, cities such as Antioch, Alexandria, Constantinople, and Rome had become important centers of the Christian religion. At the same time, however, great differences in outlook were developing between the Church in the East and the Church in the West. Things came to a head in 1054 when the two branches of the Church finally split. The Church in the East has maintained a fierce independence ever since.

THE CHURCH IN THE EAST

The Orthodox Church has about 170 million followers worldwide, with each of its Churches being self-governing [autocephalous]. Most of the Orthodox Churches are found in Eastern Europe, the Mediterranean, and the Middle East. Each of the Churches is led by a senior bishop called a "Patriarch." Among the different Patriarchs special honor is given to the Patriarch of Constantinople [the Ecumenical Patriarch] who is the "spiritual leader" of the whole Orthodox community. The two broad families into which the Orthodox Church has been traditionally divided are as follows:

✤ The Oriental Orthodox Church, which includes the Syrian, Coptic, and Ethiopian Orthodox Churches. This branch has about 30 million members.
✤ The Eastern Orthodox Church, which includes the Russian, Bulgarian, Serbian, and Greek Orthodox Churches. This family of the Church has a worldwide membership of about 130 million followers.

In Britain there are about 400,000 people who worship in an Orthodox church, but in the United States there are about 3,500,000 adherents - more than the Episcopalians, Presbyterians, and Congregationalists. A Russian Orthodox cathedral was established at Sitka, Alaska, as early as 1794.

ORTHODOX BELIEFS

The basic belief of Orthodoxy is implied in its name - "orthos" meaning "rightly" and "doxazein" meaning "glorify." Orthodox believers are those who see themselves as "rightly glorifying" God since they represent the most original form of Christianity - the traditions and practices of the united Church before it divided into its Eastern and Western forms.

Orthodox beliefs are drawn from the twin sources of the Holy Scriptures and Church tradition. All Orthodox Christians believe that:

✤ God is a Trinity. It was this that lay at the heart of the split between East and West. The argument was whether, within the Creeds of the Church, it should be said that the Spirit "proceeds from the Father" [the Orthodox form] or "from the Father and the Son" [the Western form]. This disagreement, which led to the split of 1054, is known as the "filioque controversy."

Archimandre Nathaniel of the Russian Orthodox Pskova-Pechorsky Monastery

"The understanding of God is the understanding of beauty. Beauty is at the heart of our monastic life. The life of prayer is a constant well of beauty. We have the beauty of music in the Holy Liturgy. The great beauty of monastic life is communal life in Christ. Living together in love, living without enmity, as peaceful with each other as one dead body is peaceful with another dead body, we are dead to enmity."

Quoted in Jim Forrest. *Pilgrim to the Russian Church.* New York: Crossroad Publishing Company. 1988. p.50.

- Jesus Christ, the second person in the Trinity, was both fully God and fully man.
- The Church is holy, spanning both heaven and earth. Jesus Christ, the Apostles, and the saints form the foundation of the Church to which all believers, alive and dead, belong.
- All worship must center around the sacraments, which the Orthodox Church prefers to call "Mysteries." There are seven such Mysteries - special vehicles of God's grace - and these are Holy Communion, Infant Baptism, Chrismation [Confirmation], Marriage, Penance, Ordination to the Priesthood, and Anointing the Sick.

- The Divine Liturgy, the most important Orthodox service, is celebrated each day and on special festivals and feast-days. This reenacts the birth, life, death, and resurrection of Jesus. For Orthodox believers the Liturgy is a "window into heaven" since its form never changes.

In Orthodox worship those taking part are encouraged to praise God with all their senses. The Divine Liturgy makes full use of drama with incense, the voice of the priest chanting the words, and the songs of the choir and people replying. All the congregational singing, incidentally, is unaccompanied. Icons [religious pictures] play an important role in Orthodox

ABOVE: *The iconostasis, a screen covered with icons, in an Orthodox church separates the holy altar from the congregation.*

worship. Worshipers pray in front of the icons, bowing and kissing them as a mark of respect.

IN THE GLOSSARY

Apostle ✣ Chrismation ✣ Confirmation
Creed ✣ Divine Liturgy
Episcopalian Church ✣ Holy Communion
Icon ✣ Iconostasis ✣ Infant Baptism
Ordination ✣ Orthodox Church
Patriarch ✣ Penance ✣ Priest
Sacrament ✣ Saint ✣ Trinity

2.4
THE ANGLICAN CHURCH

In 597 C.E. Pope Leo I sent the monk Augustine from Rome to bring the Christian Gospel to England. When he landed he was astonished to discover that the Gospel was already well established. The form it took, however, was very different from the highly disciplined Christianity of Rome. Augustine found a Celtic form of the faith that kept close to nature, the seasons, and the earth. Inevitably there was great suspicion between these two very different expressions of the faith. Eventually, though, the Roman form prevailed and Christians in England reluctantly accepted the authority of the Pope at the Synod of Whitby held in 664 C.E.

THE ESPECIAL PROTECTOR

The Church in England continued to recognize the authority of the Pope in Rome until 1534 when King Henry VIII declared himself to be the "Especial Protector" and head of the Church in England. This action was the result of a quarrel between the king and the Pope, who would not grant him a divorce from his wife, Catherine of Aragon. Two Acts of Parliament, in 1536 and 1539, brought about the dissolution of the monasteries - the real seat of the Pope's power in England. It was claimed that the monasteries were corrupt but the real reason for their dissolution was that their wealth was needed to ease King Henry's financial problems.

Although many traditional Catholic practices continued, Protestant ideas began to gain ground in England. Publications filtered through from Protestant Europe where Martin Luther had challenged the power of the Pope. These influenced the decision to place a copy of the English translation of the Bible by Miles Coverdale in every parish church.

> #### Henry VIII declared himself to be
>
> *"Especial Protector, only and supreme lord, and, as far as the law of Christ allows, even supreme head of the Church."*

It was Elizabeth I, though, who made the Church of England the Established Church, with its leaders, such as the Archbishop of Canterbury, being appointed by the Prime Minister. This remains the case today and distinguishes the Church of England from all other Protestant Churches. The Archbishop of Canterbury officiates on State occasions, and bishops sit in the House of Lords. In 1662 the Book of Common Prayer, after three revisions, became the official prayer book of the Church of England. In 1980 the Alternative Service Book was also authorized for use.

THE EPISCOPAL CHURCH

The teaching and practices of the Church of England soon began to spread throughout the world. In other countries the Church of England was called the Anglican Church. Everywhere that it became established the Anglican Church relied on an episcopalian form of government, with bishops exercising authority over churches in their diocese. The first Anglican Church was established in the United States in 1607, but it was not until after the War of Independence and the break with England that the Episcopal Church was established. The Episcopal Church now has about 2,500,000 members in the United States.

LEFT: *Most of the older Church of England buildings were taken over from the Roman Catholic Church at the time of the Reformation - so the two denominations have many features in common in their church buildings.*

BELIEFS

A statement drawn up in the 16th century, called the Thirty-Nine Articles, still forms the basis of belief in the Anglican Church. The Lambeth Conference [a meeting of Anglican leaders that takes place every ten years] reduced these beliefs, in 1888, to just four as follows:

✢ That the Holy Scriptures [the Bible] contain "all things necessary to salvation." This was the distinguishing mark of the Reformation and the Anglican Church is a "Reformed" Church.

✢ That the Creeds [the Nicene and Apostles'] contain all that an Anglican needs to believe.

✢ That just two sacraments [Holy Communion and Baptism] should be celebrated.

✢ That bishops are appointed by God to have special authority within the Anglican Church.

IN THE GLOSSARY

Alternative Service Book
Anglican Church ✢ Apostles' Creed
Archbishop of Canterbury
Baptism ✢ Bible ✢ Bishop
Book of Common Prayer
Church of England ✢ Creed
Episcopacy ✢ Episcopalian Church
Holy Communion ✢ Monastery
Nicene Creed ✢ Pope ✢ Protestant
Reformation ✢ Thirty-Nine Articles

2.5
THE PROTESTANT CHURCHES

A number of Protestant Churches grew out of the Church of England and other Churches from the 17th century onward. These Churches were formed because their members could not agree with the teachings of the Church of England - they could not "conform" to them. After the Act of Uniformity, which was passed by Parliament in 1662, demanded strict observance of the Book of Common Prayer, about 2,000 clergy were ejected from the Church of England and lasting divisions within the Church resulted.

THE PRESBYTERIANS

Presbyterianism is a form of church government in which the Church is governed and ruled by "presbyters" - elders. The Presbyterian Church, dating back to the 16th and 17th centuries, has always been strongest in Scotland and depends on:

❖ the supreme authority of the Bible.
❖ the importance of local church government.
❖ a simple form of worship based on readings from the Bible, hymns, spoken prayers, and a sermon explaining a biblical passage.

In 1972 the Presbyterian Church in England united with the Congregational Church of England and Wales to form the United Reformed Church.

Today the Presbyterian Church numbers about three million worshipers in the United States.

THE QUAKERS
[*Society of Friends*]

The founder of the Quakers, George Fox, wanted his followers to return to the simple faith and worship of the early Christians. He called it the Society of Friends because he wanted his followers to be friends with Jesus and each other. They were called "Quakers" by a judge who, at Fox's trial in 1650, was told to "tremble [quake] at the voice of the Lord." Throughout the years Quaker worship has been based on silence interrupted only by those speaking under the inspiration of the Spirit. The Society of Friends does not have a Creed which all of its members must accept since that would restrict true religion. There are no ministers nor do the Quakers celebrate any of the sacraments.

The Quakers refuse to do military service, which has often led to conflict between Quakers and the law.

THE BAPTISTS

In 1612 the first Baptist Church was opened in London and was firmly based on the principle that only adult believers in Christ should be baptized. Infant Baptism - the practice of the Roman Catholic Church and the Church of England - was firmly ruled out because it was seen as

Nicolas Cabasila. Life in Christ

"To be baptized is to be born according to Christ; it is to receive existence, to come into being out of nothing."

unscriptural. The Baptists were persecuted in the 17th century but have since become a worldwide denomination with about 40 million members. Over 15 million alone belong to the Southern Baptists in the United States.

RIGHT: The Salvation Army is very visible as a spiritual and social agency in many different countries.

Wesley's Conversion

On May 24, 1738 John Wesley went to a society in Aldersgate Street where someone was reading Luther's Preface to the Epistle to the Romans. Wesley described in his Journal what happened at exactly "a quarter before nine":

"I felt my heart strangely warmed. I felt I did trust in Christ, Christ alone, for salvation; and an assurance was given me that he had taken away my sins, even mine, and saved me from the law of sin and death."

THE METHODISTS

Methodism came into existence through the teaching and preaching of an Anglican clergyman, John Wesley [1703-91]. The name "Methodist" was applied to Wesley and his friends because of the "methodical" way they approached the Bible. A "heart-warming" spiritual experience convinced Wesley that God had taken away his sins. He traveled across Britain and the United States preaching to vast crowds and founding many communities of believers. He is thought to have traveled more than 100,000 miles on horseback in England alone.

In America, though, it was George Whitefield, one of the founders of Methodism in the 18th century, who had the greatest impact. In the United States the United Methodist Church has over 9,000,000 worshipers.

THE SALVATION ARMY

During the 19th century a new religious force appeared in England with the foundation of the Salvation Army by William Booth, a Methodist minister, in 1878. Working in the poor areas of England Booth set up an organization run along military lines with a general [initially Booth himself], colonels, adjutants, and corporals. Two years later the Salvation Army adopted its distinctive uniform and made use of brass bands, and testimonies, in its open-air witness. Within a few years the Army spread from London to other towns as well as spreading its work overseas. Between 1940 and 1995 the Salvation Army more than doubled its membership in the United States and now totals 450,000. Today the Salvation Army has workers in 74 countries.

Members of the Salvation Army meet for worship in a citadel. The name itself suggests a place of refuge for those inside from the wicked world around. Music plays a very important part in such worship and members of the congregation are encouraged to participate in the rousing hymns. Along with the Quakers, the Salvation Army is the only Christian denomination that does not celebrate any of the sacraments.

IN THE GLOSSARY

Baptism ✦ Baptist Church ✦ Bible
Book of Common Prayer
Church of England ✦ Citadel ✦ Creed
Free Church ✦ Infant Baptism
Methodist Church ✦ Nonconformist
Presbyterian Church ✦ Protestant
Quakers ✦ Roman Catholic Church
Sacraments ✦ Salvation Army
Society of Friends
United Reformed Church

2.6
CHURCHES IN AMERICA

The situation of Christianity in the United States is both unique and complex. Historical reasons have prevented any one Christian denomination from gaining the upper hand because the numerous immigrant groups have brought their own religious preferences and allegiances with them. The First Amendment of the Constitution guaranteed not only real religious freedom of worship but also genuine equality for all religious faiths together with the absence of official government support for any one of them. As a result the panorama of Christian denominations throughout the United States is very wide indeed.

THE BAPTISTS

Baptists form the largest grouping of Protestants in the United States. The Southern Baptist Convention numbers 15.2 million members; the American Baptist Church has 1.5 million members; and the two National Baptist Churches claim to have 11 million followers between them. In total the number of Baptists is around 30 million - the largest of all Church groupings in the United States except for the Roman Catholic Church. Although the Southern Baptists have differences based largely on geographical regions, almost all American Baptists insist that the Bible is without error [inerrant] and this belief underpins

RIGHT: In the Baptist Church, Baptism is performed only when a believer has experienced personal faith in Jesus Christ.

John Cotton. The True Constitution of a Particular Visible Church [1642]

"As for Baptism, it is to be dispensed by a Minister of the Word unto a Believer professing his Repentance and his Faith."

all of their worship and belief. Baptists follow a strict code of moral behavior and are strongly opposed to such practices as abortion. The most successful worldwide preacher of the 20th century has been the Southern Baptist Billy Graham, whose fundamentalist message has made extensive use of radio and television.

Believer's Baptism has always been the main distinguishing mark of the Baptist Church. Baptists argue that a person cannot be baptized unless they have shown a personal faith in Jesus Christ. This faith is born within them when they are "converted" and saved through the death and resurrection of Jesus.

METHODISM

As we saw in section 2.5, Methodism grew out of the preaching of John Wesley and others in England during the 18th century. In the United States the Methodist Church, totaling almost 30 million members, includes the United Methodist Church [nine million], the Free Methodists, and two Black-led Methodist Churches. In its early years Methodism soon became dominant in the small towns of the South and Midwest. As it did so, however, it became less evangelistic and such groups as the Free Methodists and the Church of the Nazarene, which wanted to retain the emphasis of Wesley on conversion and holy living, broke away to form their own Churches.

THE LUTHERAN CHURCH

In the 1840s German and Scandinavian immigration took place on a very wide scale into the United States. These were the countries where the Lutheran religion was

strongest, so naturally the immigrants brought their religion with them. Many small Lutheran Churches were formed - as many as 64 at one time. The largest Lutheran Church, the Evangelical Lutheran Church in America, with over 5 million members, was formed through a merger in 1987. The Lutheran Church - Missouri Synod, with almost 3 million members – is a more conservative Church. Worship in the country's Lutheran churches is usually sedate with a great emphasis upon beautiful music and learned, scholarly sermons.

THE ROMAN CATHOLIC CHURCH

The Roman Catholic Church claims to have 58 million members [about 25% of the total population] in the United States. There was a major expansion of the Catholic Church throughout the United States in the years following World War II. Between 1945 and 1949 the Roman Catholic Church was baptizing somewhere in the region of one million babies a year. Catholic schools and colleges were rapidly coming into

ABOVE: The Methodist Church is one of the largest denominations in the United States.

existence. In 1960 the election of the country's first Catholic President, John F. Kennedy, showed how much progress the Church had made. Catholics in the United States welcomed the Second Vatican Council [1962-65] as an open indication of the Church's willingness to bring "church" into the daily lives of the parishioners.

The Council also encouraged important discussions with other Churches - especially the Lutherans. Yet, in 1968 when the encyclical on birth control, called *Humanae Vitae*, was published millions of Roman Catholics, for the first time in the Church's history, chose to ignore its teachings.

IN THE GLOSSARY

Baptist Church ✦ Believer's Baptism
Bible ✦ Lutheran Church
Methodist Church ✦ Protestant Church
Roman Catholic Church

2.7
THE EVANGELICALS

Within most major Christian denominations there are streams or tendencies of churchmanship. Anglo-Catholics, for instance, are members of Anglican/Episcopal Churches who place a Roman Catholic emphasis on their beliefs and worship. Liberals are those Christians who believe that their faith must change as times change. Evangelicals are those Christians who believe that the Bible provides the only authority for the Christian life. In the aftermath of World War II the Anglo-Catholic tendency was strongest, but since the late 1960s, the Evangelicals have gained the ascendancy. About 25% of all Christians are now thought to be Evangelical believers.

EVANGELICAL BELIEFS

There are Evangelicals in all of the major Protestant denominations and their beliefs are more clearly defined than those of any other Christian group. Evangelicals believe in placing the Bible at the center of all worship and Christian living. For

2 Timothy 3.15,16

"You know who your teachers were, and you remember that ever since you were a child, you have known the Holy Scriptures, which are able to give you the wisdom that leads to salvation through faith in Christ Jesus. All Scripture is inspired by God and is useful for teaching the truth, rebuking error, correcting faults, and giving instruction for right living, so that the person who serves God may be fully qualified and equipped to do every kind of good deed."

them the Bible is inspired, faultless, and inerrant [without error]. Evangelicals believe that when the books of the Bible were first being written the writers were inspired by the Holy Spirit to write down "the Word of God." Therefore, when people read the Bible today, God speaks to them. In Evangelical services great emphasis is placed on the reading of the Bible and also on the sermon - in which a passage from the Bible is explained by the priest or minister. Evangelicals believe that when the Bible is preached, in the power of the Holy Spirit, it is able to remind those listening of their own sinfulness and God's power to forgive.

Because of their very high regard for the Bible, Evangelicals spend much time reading and studying it. They usually set aside time each day to pray and find ways to put the teachings of the Bible into practice [called a "Quiet Time"]. They also meet together regularly with other believers to

ABOVE: *Evangelicals stress the importance for all Christians of spending time reading the Bible for themselves. To help them to do this, Bible-reading notes are produced.*

study the Bible. Special study-groups are held regularly in church or in people's homes to help them to understand the Bible better. In the Anglican Church, for instance, special Bible-study sessions are often held during Lent as part of the preparation for the coming of Easter. The Bible itself encourages believers to read and

ABOVE: Evangelicals often use rousing music as part of their church services in order to express their enthusiasm for their Christian faith.

✢ ✢ ✢

EVANGELICAL CREED OUTSIDE A CHURCH:

✢ ✢ ✢

About Ourselves: Every person is a sinner by nature and therefore separated from God and under his judgment. God invites every person to turn from their sin and trust in Jesus Christ as Savior. All who believe in him are saved, but those who do not turn to him in repentance and faith remain under God's judgment.

About the Bible: The Bible is God's living Word and is therefore totally true. Through it He speaks to the world today. It contains all that we need to know about God and about how we can be made right with him and live to please him.

IN THE GLOSSARY

Anglican ✢ Anglo-Catholic
Bible ✢ Easter
Episcopalian Church
Evangelical ✢ Holy Spirit ✢ Lent
Minister ✢ Priest ✢ Sermon

study it. A belief in the Bible tells us all that we need to know about God - and ourselves:
✢ Humankind was created by God.
✢ Every human being is born with a sinful nature [called "Original Sin"] and because of this nature everyone stands under the condemnation of God.

✢ God, in his mercy, sent Jesus to be the Savior of the world.
✢ Christ died "in our place" and took the sins of everyone on himself.
✢ Those who respond to God's message are forgiven and those who do not are condemned to eternal punishment.
✢ The same Jesus who died to save everyone will return to the world at some time in the future to be its Judge [called "the Second Coming"]. Evangelicals believe that being "converted" is the start of the Christian

life. The converted are then expected to share their new life with others and this is called "evangelism." Evangelism can take place through large rallies or meetings, in church services, on the streets, in the work-place, or in the home. Whatever the chosen method Evangelicals are constantly seeking to introduce other people to Jesus.

2.8
THE CHARISMATIC MOVEMENT

Since the late 1960s many Protestant and Roman Catholic Churches, in Britain and the United States, have been greatly affected by the Charismatic Movement. This movement emphasizes the role of the Holy Spirit in giving Christians an intense experience of God. This experience is expressed through such activities as prophecy, speaking in tongues, healing through the laying on of hands, and the performance of spiritual miracles. Belief and religious authority are less important in charismatic groups than direct spiritual experience.

1 Corinthians 12. 8-10

"The Spirit's presence is shown in some way in each person for the good of all. The Spirit gives one person a message full of wisdom, while to another person the same Spirit gives a message full of knowledge. One and the same Spirit gives faith to one person, while to another person he gives the power to heal. The Spirit gives one person the power to work miracles; to another, the gift of speaking God's message; and to yet another, the ability to tell the difference between gifts that come from the Spirit and those that do not. To one person he gives the ability to speak in strange tongues and to another he gives the ability to explain what is said. But it is one and the same Spirit who does all this…"

THE CHARISMATIC MOVEMENT

The Pentecostal Movement is thought to have begun in a small church in Los Angeles in 1906. Christians there experienced what came to be known as "the baptism in the Spirit" and were speaking in tongues and prophesying. When the movement spread to Britain it began in the Anglican Church but soon spread much wider. The following two Churches were formed to foster the Pentecostal approach:

a. THE ASSEMBLIES OF GOD, in 1924, with an emphasis on self-government in each church.

b. THE ELIM CHURCH, formed in 1926, emphasizing a central form of church government.

For a long time these intense religious experiences stayed largely within the Pentecostal Movement but in the early 1960s Christians in other denominations began to claim that they too had received the gifts of the Spirit. The Charismatic Movement was born.

THE GIFTS OF THE SPIRIT

What "gifts" are we speaking about? When the Christian Church was born on the Day of Pentecost the first disciples felt the power of God come on them, giving them the courage to go out and speak of Jesus. On that day they also spoke in the different languages of the people gathered to listen to them in Jerusalem. This was the first recorded example of "speaking in tongues." From 1 Corinthians 12.1-11 we learn about the different gifts which, according to Paul, God had given the Church. Among them were

a. HEALING. Healing meetings are common services in Charismatic churches. Prayers are said for those who are ill and hands laid on them so that their health might be restored.

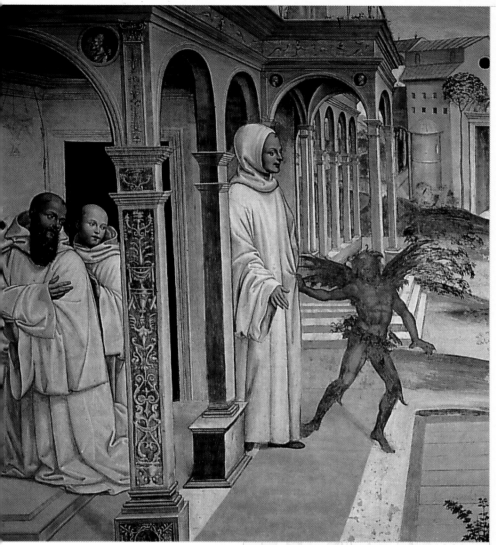

⊹ ⊹ ⊹

SATANIC POWERS

⊹ ⊹ ⊹

At the heart of all Charismatic Christianity are two basic beliefs:

a. That God is sovereign and almighty. The gifts are God's to give – and he gives them only to the people he chooses.

b. That Satan, the Devil, has a more limited power. Charismatics are convinced that people can be controlled by demons today just as they were in the time of Jesus. God, though, has given people in the Church the power to cast out [exorcise] these demons. According to Charismatic teaching there is a close link between these demons and sickness. There are some people with the gift of healing, as Paul promised, and this takes place through the laying of hands on the head of the sick person. Those who have this gift often find themselves fighting against the powers of darkness before they bring wholeness to a person.

b. PROPHECY. People in Charismatic churches pass on God's message to others in the congregation. The message can concern the past, the present, or the future. **c.** SPEAKING IN TONGUES. Used in both private and public prayer when a person finds himself or herself praising God in an unknown language.

There are other gifts of the Spirit mentioned in the New Testament. These include the gifts of faith, interpretation,

ABOVE: Exorcisms are a part of the worship of those churches within the Charismatic Movement. Christians from such churches believe that a person can be possessed by demons and that these demons need to be expelled if the person is to be made whole.

wisdom, teaching, and discernment. Whatever the gift given by God it is intended for just one reason - to be used for the benefit of the local church.

IN THE GLOSSARY

Anglican Church ⊹ Assemblies of God
Charismatic Movement
Day of Pentecost ⊹ Devil ⊹ Disciples
Elim Church ⊹ Exorcism ⊹ Holy Spirit
Jerusalem ⊹ New Testament ⊹ Paul
Protestant ⊹ Roman Catholic Church
Satan ⊹ Speaking in tongues

THE
SCRIPTURES

*"The English Bible, a book which,
if everything else in our language
should perish, would alone suffice
to show the whole extent of its
beauty and power."*

T.B. MACAULAY. ESSAYS
AND BIOGRAPHIES:
JOHN DRYDEN [1828]

3.1
THE BIBLE

The Bible, the holy book for all Christians, is actually a collection of books divided into two parts - the Old Testament and the New Testament. In addition to the 66 books of the Bible, Roman Catholics also include the Apocrypha. In the Jerusalem Bible there are seven books from the Apocrypha. The Orthodox Church follows the Catholic canon but adds a further five books to the Apocrypha. Protestants do not believe that these books carry the authority of Scripture.

THE OLD TESTAMENT

The early Christians were almost all Jews, so they were very familiar with the Jewish Scriptures. The same Scriptures are included in the Christian Bible although in a different order. Christians refer to this part of their Bible as "the Old Testament" but Jews find this offensive because it suggests that their Scriptures are largely obsolete. The books in the Jewish Scriptures are divided into three sections:

1. THE BOOKS OF THE LAW [THE TORAH]. The first five books of the Bible - Genesis, Exodus, Leviticus, Numbers, and Deuteronomy - contain the most important elements of the Jewish faith. They begin with the story of the creation of the world and the formation of the Jewish nation under Abraham. Then follows the account of the delivery of the Israelites from Jewish slavery [an event called the Exodus] under the leadership of Moses, who also received the Law, including the Ten Commandments, from God on Mount Sinai. The hurried exit of the Israelites from Egypt and their arrival

Justin Martyr c.155 C.E.

"The memoirs of the Apostles or the writings of the prophets are read [in worship] as long as time permits."

40 years later in the Promised Land of Canaan are celebrated by Jews each year in their Passover [Pesach] festival.

2. THE PROPHETS. A "prophet" was a man or woman who delivered the message of God to the people. There are many books in the Old Testament containing the messages of different prophets, although none of them were written by the prophets themselves. These books are divided into two sections:

✤ the major Prophets. Three prophets - Isaiah, Jeremiah, and Ezekiel - have substantial books named after them.
✤ the minor Prophets. There are 12 books at the very end of the Old Testament that convey the words of the so-called minor prophets - including Amos, Hosea, and Micah.

3. THE WRITINGS. These books include the Psalms, Proverbs, and Ecclesiastes.

The books of the Old Testament were probably written over a period of about 3,000 years, running from the story of the Jewish people around 2000 B.C.E. through to the years preceding the Roman occupation of Palestine in 63 B.C.E.

THE NEW TESTAMENT

The 27 books of the New Testament tell the story of Jesus and the early Christian Church - from the birth of Jesus through to the deaths of Peter and Paul in 64 C.E. Most of the books were written within a generation or two of the death of Jesus, and they include the following:

1. THE LETTERS OR EPISTLES OF PAUL, PETER, JAMES, JOHN, AND OTHERS. These are the oldest writings in the New Testament. Most of them explain the importance of the death and resurrection of Jesus for those living the Christian life.

2. THE FOUR GOSPELS - Matthew, Mark, Luke, and John - which provide us with our only real information about the birth,

life, and death of Jesus. Three of the Gospels - Matthew, Mark, and Luke - are called "The Synoptic Gospels" because they present a broadly similar picture of Jesus. They also share much of their material with each other. The first of

T.B. Macaulay. Essays and Biographies: John Dryden [1828]

"The English Bible, a book which, if everything else in our language should perish, would alone suffice to show the whole extent of its beauty and power."

them, Mark, was written about 65 C.E. with the other two following soon afterward. The fourth Gospel, John's, takes a very different approach to Jesus and was written later.

3. THE HISTORY OF THE EARLY CHRISTIAN CHURCH AFTER JESUS HAD LEFT THE EARTH. This is recorded in the Acts of the Apostles and is believed to have been written by the same author who wrote Luke's Gospel.

4. PROPHECY. The last book in the New Testament is called Revelation, which is a highly symbolic description of the end of the world.

ABOVE: *Among holy books the Bible is unique since it contains texts that are sacred in two religions - Judaism and Christianity.*

IN THE GLOSSARY

Abraham ✣ Acts of the Apostles
Apocrypha ✣ Bible ✣ Exodus
Gospel ✣ Jerusalem Bible ✣ Luke
Mark ✣ Matthew ✣ Moses
New Testament ✣ Old Testament
Orthodox Church ✣ Paul ✣ Peter
Pesach ✣ Prophet ✣ Protestant
Synoptic Gospels
Ten Commandments ✣ Torah

3.2
PUTTING THE BIBLE TOGETHER

Every religion has its own collection of holy writings that it considers to be authoritative and inspired. The collection itself is called a "canon" [from the Greek word meaning "measuring rod"], providing the standard against which all teaching and behavior in that religion can be tested. The 66 books contained in the Bible were all chosen because they were seen to be holy books whose authority the Jewish faith and the Christian Church could accept.

To begin with the Church accepted the Jewish Scriptures because it believed that they all pointed to the coming of God's Messiah - Jesus. Most of the early Christians had, in any case, been taught, as Jews, to treat these Scriptures as divine. Although the Jewish Canon was not finally established until the Synod of Jamnia in 90 C.E. there was general agreement about the contents of the Jewish Scriptures by the time of Jesus.

Louis B. Meyer

"The number one book of the ages was written by a committee and it was called the Bible."

THE BOOKS OF
THE NEW TESTAMENT

The early Christian writers scoured the pages of the Jewish Scriptures for evidence to support their claim that Jesus was the Jewish Messiah. The most prolific of these writers was Paul who sent many letters to

churches that he had founded and to individual Christians. The first of these letters preserved in the New Testament, 1 Thessalonians, was probably written around 49 C.E. and this was about 16 years after Jesus had been put to death. Paul was a tireless missionary, traveling throughout the Roman Empire until he was put to death by the Emperor Nero in 64 C.E.

The Gospels were written after the Epistles. The first written account of the life of Jesus that still exists is Mark's Gospel - written about 40 years after the death of Jesus. In between these two events, however, the information about Jesus had been kept alive in the memories, conversations, and preaching of those people who believed. Mark's Gospel was soon followed by Matthew's and Luke's accounts between 70 and 80 C.E. Then, toward the end of the first century, John composed his own highly individual account of the ministry of Jesus. At the end of his life the same author found himself on the isle of Patmos, where he

had the bizarre vision of heaven that is contained in the Book of Revelation - the final book of the New Testament. We

John Bunyan. Grace Abounding to the Chief of Sinners

"I have sometimes seen more in a line of the Bible than I could well tell how to stand under, yet at another time the whole Bible hath been to me as dry as a stick."

cannot be sure if the same person wrote the three letters that also bear John's name. By the end of the first century C.E. most, if not all, of the books of the New Testament had been written.

Samuel Taylor Coleridge

"I have found in the Bible words for my inmost thoughts, songs for my joy, utterance for my hidden griefs and pleadings for my shame and feebleness."

✛ ✛ ✛

THE CANON OF THE NEW TESTAMENT

✛ ✛ ✛

For a long time the books written by the Apostles and other Church leaders were very highly valued in the early Christian Churches. Although no attempt was made to bring them together they obviously circulated very widely. By the end of the second century most of the books of the New Testament were accepted as being special although there was disagreement over one or two of them. In 367 Athanasius, an influential leader in the Eastern Church, set out his Canon containing 27 books and this was confirmed at the Synod of Carthage in 397. Altogether it was accepted that the Christian Bible should contain 66 books and that is the way it has remained ever since. The Roman Catholic Church accepted this decision although it did not formally accept the Canon of Scripture until the Council of Trent in the 16th century.

RIGHT: The Bible starts with the story of the creation of the world and the placing of the first man and woman in the Garden of Eden. No one knows how old these stories are, or who wrote them.

IN THE GLOSSARY

Apostle ✛ Bible ✛ Canon
Epistle ✛ Gospel ✛ Gospels
John ✛ Luke ✛ Mark ✛ Matthew
Messiah ✛ New Testament
Paul ✛ Roman Catholic Church

3.3
TRANSLATING THE BIBLE

The bulk of the Old Testament was originally written in Hebrew, while the New Testament was in Greek. During the third century B.C.E. the Old Testament was translated into Greek. This was called the Septuagint; its name stems from the fact that 72 scholars are believed to have taken 72 days to translate it. The translations were identical although the scholars worked alone! The Septuagint was intended for Jews who had been "dispersed" across the ancient world and so did not know any Hebrew.

INTO LATIN

Although the documents of the New Testament were written in Greek, Jesus actually spoke in Aramaic. There are just a few traces of this language remaining in the New Testament. Soon, however, Latin became the official language of the Western Church, and a Latin translation of the Bible, the Vulgate, became the only one that Western Christians were allowed to use. The translation was made by St. Jerome at the request of Pope Damascus. He completed the Gospels in 384 and the whole Bible was completed in 404. The Council of Trent [1545-63] called this version of the Bible the undisputed Word of God but few people could read or understand Latin.

INTO ENGLISH

There were two important events that greatly affected the translation of the Bible:
1. THE INVENTION OF PRINTING AROUND 1450. Instead of being copied by hand the Bible could now be printed.

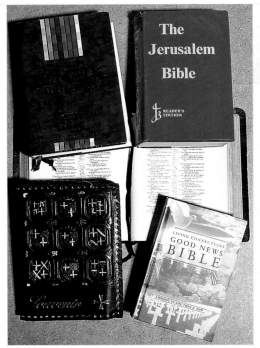

2. THE BEGINNING OF THE PROTESTANT REFORMATION FROM 1517 ONWARD. This upheaval in the Church was inspired by the Bible and gave the Reformers a desire to place the Bible in as many hands as possible - in a language that people could understand.

LEFT: *The Bible was originally written in Hebrew and Greek, but today there are many different version and translations of the Bible.*

David Ben-Gurion (1886–1973), Israeli Prime Minister

"I was reading the Bible in many different languages and I saw that it cannot really be translated, the real meaning cannot be given in another language. It is only in Hebrew that you feel the full meaning of it - all the associations which a different word has."

The translation and printing of the Bible into English became imperative. William Tyndale [1494-1536] saw the ignorance of the Bible's teaching among clergy and laity alike. He moved to Antwerp, in Belgium, and began to print the New Testament in English from 1525 onward. Under incredibly difficult conditions of secrecy he published a translation that was both accurate and in the language of the people.

William Tyndale

"...it is impossible to establish the lay people in any truth, except the Scriptures are plainly laid before their eyes in the mother tongue."

Just before Tyndale died in prison a translation of the whole Bible into English, the Miles Coverdale version, was circulating. In 1539 the Great Bible was placed, by royal decree, in every parish church in England. The Geneva Bible, published in 1560 by a group of Protestant exiles in Geneva, was the first translation of the whole Bible directly from the original Hebrew and Greek.

In 1611 all existing translations were superseded by the Authorized Version. It proved to be so popular that it went unchallenged for three centuries. Forty-seven scholars, under the inspiration of King James I of England, used all the existing translations in many lamnguages and made constant reference to the original texts. The feel of the translators for poetry and rhythm meant that the new translation was eminently suitable for reading in public. It still is.

In the 20th century many private translations, including one of the New Testament by J.B. Phillips, were made into modern English. The complete Revised Standard Version was published in 1952, while the Jerusalem Bible appeared in 1966 and has been used by many Catholics ever since. Evangelicals published several translations including the ever-popular Good News Bible, with its unusual illustrations, which was

published between 1966 and 1976. The New English Bible was published in 1970 to be replaced, in 1989, by the Revised English Bible.

The British and Foreign Bible Society [now simply the "Bible Society"] and the

ABOVE: Before the invention of mechanical printing methods, monks copied and illustrated the Bible by hand.

IN THE GLOSSARY

Aramaic ✣ Authorized Version
Bible ✣ Council of Trent
Good News Version
Jerusalem Bible
New Testament
Old Testament ✣ Protestant
Reformation
Septuagint ✣ Vulgate

Wycliffe Bible Translators have been laboring to translate the Bible into as many different languages as possible. Parts of the Bible are now to be found in more than 500 different languages although the work of translating the Bible still continues at a rapid rate.

During the last 50 years there has been an explosion of different versions of the Bible. Except for those, such as the Jerusalem Bible, that are strictly denominational, most of the versions have come from Evangelical translators.

3.4
USING THE BIBLE

The Bible, as we have seen, was brought together over a long period of time to provide a kind of "inspirational warehouse" for Christian believers to use. Both individual believers and worshiping communities draw constantly from its well of inspiration. The Bible shows the wide variety of ways in which God has been understood and the struggles that people have endured to make sense of their religious experiences.

THE VALUE OF THE BIBLE

While some Christians, most notably Evangelicals, would claim that the whole Bible was inspired by God they would not claim that all parts are equally valuable. Few Christians, for example, would find the list of tribes that emerged from Egyptian slavery [Numbers 26] or the disreputable exploits of some Old Testament kings to be spiritually nourishing. They would also acknowledge that many parts of the Bible reflect the standards and values of antiquity - not those of today. To take just two examples:

1. IT IS ASSUMED THROUGHOUT THE BIBLE THAT THERE WILL BE SLAVES AND SLAVE-OWNERS. The morality of keeping slaves is never discussed. When an escaped slave, Onesimus, approached Paul in prison to ask for his advice he was told to return to his slave-owner.

RIGHT: St. Benedict, who established the Benedictine Order of monks, is shown here reading the Bible.

2. FROM THE OPENING CHAPTERS OF THE BIBLE, WHICH STATE THAT THE WOMAN WAS CREATED FROM THE RIBS OF THE MAN, WOMEN ARE GIVEN A SECONDARY ROLE. In the relationship between a man and a woman Paul suggests that a wife should be subordinate and obey her husband.

Yet, in contrast, many parts of the Bible contain insights into matters that are of timeless concern and interest. The Ten Commandments [Exodus 20.1-17] and the Beatitudes [Matthew 5.1-12] are just two examples of passages that lay down timeless principles. One of the main tasks for the Church today is to help Christians discover just what the message of the Bible is for them, and the world, today.

THE BIBLE IN USE

In spite of the problems of some of the advice given in the Bible, it has always been a great source of inspiration for

Debatable advice from the Bible

"Slaves, obey your human masters with fear and trembling; and do it with a sincere heart, as though you were serving Christ."
[Ephesians 6.5]

"Wives, submit to your husbands as to the Lord. For a husband has authority over his wife just as Christ has authority over the Church…"
[Ephesians 5.22,23]

The question of authority is one of the most important in the modern Christian Church. In both the Roman Catholic and Orthodox Churches authority has always resided in two places:

a. The traditions of the Church and, for Roman Catholics, the Pope.
b. The Holy Scriptures.

Since the Reformation the basic principle of Protestants has been to stand on the authority of the Bible alone. In practice, though, neither approach has been without its problems. The traditions and teachings of the Church have sometimes conflicted with the teachings of the Bible. The Bible is a diverse collection of teachings that do not present a coherent system of belief. There have been many arguments among Christians in the past over just what the Bible does, and does not, say.

Christian believers. The use of the Bible is a central part of all Christian worship; passages are regularly read and used as the basis for sermons. Over a given period of time the bulk of the Bible is read in public in most churches. In most church services there are two [Old Testament and New Testament] or three [Old

ABOVE: For many Christians, reading the Bible is a very important part of their personal spiritual development.

Testament, New Testament, and Epistles] readings from the Bible. Most Christians also read the Bible systematically and regularly as an important part of their own spiritual devotions.

In Roman Catholic and Orthodox churches the Gospel reading is carried out, by a priest, from the centre of the church. This is to underline the great importance of this part of the Bible.

Martin Luther, the Protestant Reformer, placing the authority of the Bible above that of the Catholic Church

"Here I stand, I can do no other!"

IN THE GLOSSARY

Anglican Church ✤ Beatitudes ✤ Bible
Easter ✤ Epistle ✤ Evangelical
Lent ✤ New Testament
Old Testament ✤ Orthodox Church
Paul ✤ Pope ✤ Protestant
Reformation ✤ Roman Catholic Church
Ten Commandments

CHAPTER FOUR

SACRAMENTS
AND
CEREMONIES

" 'Twas God the Word that spake it,
He took the Bread and brake it;
And what the word did make it;
That I believe, and take it. "

4.1
THE SACRAMENTS

The sacraments stand at the heart of worship for all Roman Catholic and Orthodox Christians, as well as for many Christians from the Anglican/Episcopalian Churches. The sacraments have a much lower profile in Protestant Churches, where they are not called sacraments. The sacraments are ceremonies or rituals that can be traced back to the ministry of Jesus or the worship of the early Church. Since then such sacraments ["mysteries"] have been used to transmit the mystery of Christ to worshipers.

THE TWO SIDES OF A SACRAMENT

There are two important ingredients to every sacrament:

1. THE PHYSICAL OR MATERIAL ELEMENT - the part of the sacrament that can be felt, touched, smelled, or tasted. During the service of Holy Communion, for example, a worshiper drinks a small quantity of wine and eats a piece of bread or a host. By using these material elements each believer is helped to enter into, and share, the death of Jesus. Similarly, in Infant Baptism, water is poured over the baby to symbolize the cleansing of the child from his or her sins.

2. THE SPIRITUAL OR INVISIBLE ELEMENT. The physical elements used in a sacrament are only important because they bring God and the worshiper closer together. The ceremonies or rituals have little value in themselves. It is the spiritual blessing that results from the sacrament that matters.

THE SACRAMENTS

Christians disagree over just how many sacraments [special channels of God's grace] there are. Roman Catholic and Orthodox Christians observe seven sacraments, although the Orthodox Church prefers to call them "Mysteries." They are

❖ the Eucharist - the ritual meal at which the death of Jesus is reenacted. In the Roman Catholic Church this is called "the Mass," while in the Orthodox Church it is "the Divine Liturgy."

❖ Infant Baptism - the initiation into the Church and the symbolic cleansing from sin of the child by water.

❖ Confirmation - the entering into full membership of the Church.

❖ Penance - the confession and forgiveness [absolution] of sins.

❖ Extreme Unction - the anointing of the sick with oil, especially those approaching death.

❖ Holy Orders - the consecration of a person as a deacon, priest, or bishop to serve the Church.

❖ Matrimony.

Protestant Churches recognize just two sacraments - Baptism and Holy Communion - since they are the only ones that can be clearly traced back to Jesus himself. Most of the Protestant Churches, notably the Baptist, prefer to call Holy Communion "the Lord's Supper" or "the Breaking of Bread" although Methodist Churches, with their Anglican roots, usually retain the old title. While most Churches baptize infants, the Baptist Church, and a few others, baptize only believing adults. Although the Anglican Church baptizes mainly children there are provisions in the Alternative Service Book for the baptism of adults. Since this requires special facilities in a church, some

---

The Book of Common Prayer. Offices of Instruction

Q. What meanest thou by this word Sacrament?

A. I mean an outward and visible sign of an inward and spiritual grace.

St Leo the Great. Sermons

"What was visible in Christ has now passed over into the sacraments of the Church."

ABOVE: *In every sacrament the physical and the spiritual are brought together. This sacrament of Holy Communion was first performed by Jesus when he offered bread and wine to the Apostles at the Last Supper.*

Elizabeth I

"'Twas God the Word that spake it,
He took the Bread and brake it;
And what the word did make it;
That I believe, and take it."

Anglican churches carry out adult baptism in the local Baptist church. The Salvation Army and the Quakers, alone among the major Christian Churches, do not celebrate any of the sacraments.

Most Christians believe that Jesus showed the power of God through his life and that this power now reaches them through the sacraments. This belief is particularly important in Churches, such as the Roman Catholic and Orthodox, that see themselves as "Sacramental Churches." In these Churches the main role of the priest is to administer the sacraments. It is through the sacraments, some Christians believe, that humankind can gain some small understanding of the communion that exists between God the Father, God the Son, and God the Holy Spirit.

IN THE GLOSSARY:

Absolution ✤ Alternative Service Book
Anglican Church ✤ Baptist Church
Bishop ✤ Book of Common Prayer
Breaking of Bread ✤ Confirmation
Deacon ✤ Divine Liturgy ✤ Eucharist
Extreme Unction ✤ Holy Communion
Holy Orders ✤ Host ✤ Mass
Lord's Supper ✤ Infant Baptism
Orthodox Church ✤ Penance ✤ Priest
Quakers ✤ Roman Catholic Church
Sacrament ✤ Salvation Army

4.2
INFANT BAPTISM

Like any other Jewish boy, Jesus was circumcised and dedicated to God in the Temple when he was just a few days old [Luke 2.21-35]. He then emerged, after many years of obscurity, to be baptized in the Jordan River by John the Baptist [Matthew 3.13-17]. Since he was 30 years old at the time of his Baptism, we are clearly talking here about adult Baptism. There is, in fact, no reference in the New Testament to Infant Baptism. It was not until the fourth century that Christian families began to have their babies baptized. This happened because the belief grew up that unbaptized babies, many of whom died in infancy, would not go to heaven.

INFANT BAPTISM

Infant Baptism is an important sacrament in Anglican/Episcopal, Roman Catholic, and Orthodox Churches. The ceremony usually takes place within the first few months of life, and in the Roman

---

The Book of Common Prayer. Articles of Religion. XXVII

"Baptism is not only a sign of profession, and mark of difference, whereby Christian men are discerned from others that be not christened, but it is also a sign of Regeneration or new Birth…The Baptism of young Children is any wise to be retained in the Church."

Catholic Church is believed to be necessary for salvation. Infant Baptism in these Churches is the way by which a baby becomes a member of the Church

[an initiation ceremony]. Not surprisingly, though, there are variations in the way that the sacrament is carried out:

1. IN THE ROMAN CATHOLIC AND ANGLICAN/EPISCOPAL SERVICES THE CHILD IS PRESENTED FOR BAPTISM BY ITS PARENTS AND GODPARENTS. The godparents promise to watch over the child's upbringing to ensure that he or she is brought up in the Christian faith. Both parents and godparents are asked to affirm their own faith in Christ by answering several questions. This is followed by the reading of a passage from the Bible on the subject of baptism. Finally the child is baptized with water being poured over him or her as the priest makes the sign of the cross and says:

"I baptize you in the name of the Father, and of the Son and of the Holy Spirit."

After the baby has been baptized a lighted candle is often handed to the parents to symbolize the movement of the child from darkness to light. The whole congregation tells the child:

"We welcome you into the Lord's family. We are members together of the body of Christ: we are children of the same Heavenly Father; we are inheritors

---

Alternative Service Book (the Church of England's modern prayer book)

"Children who are too young to profess the faith are baptised on the understanding that they are brought up as Christians within the family of the Church."

---

together of the Kingdom of God."

Christian parents believe that this ceremony marks the spiritual rebirth of the child as others renounce all evil and repent on its behalf. The child can return much later, at Confirmation, to make the same vows for himself or herself.

ABOVE: *The word "baptism" was originally
applied to sheep who were dipped in water to kill
any parasites. When applied to the Church ritual
the same idea was carried forward - the dipping
of people under the water.*

IN THE GLOSSARY

Alternative Service Book
Anglican Church ❖ Baptism
Bible ❖ Book of Common Prayer
Chrism ❖ Chrismation
Circumcision ❖ Confirmation
Holy Spirit ❖ Infant Baptism
John the Baptist ❖ Matthew
New Testament ❖ Ordination
Orthodox Church
Roman Catholic Church ❖ Temple

2. THE ORTHODOX CHURCH. In an Orthodox Church Baptism and Confirmation [Chrismation] follow each other in the same service, which is usually carried out when the baby is eight days old. After blessing the water in the font with a prayer, and breathing on it, the priest anoints the baby with the "oil of gladness." The baby is placed in the font facing eastward - the direction of the rising sun and a symbol of new life. The baby is then completely undressed and immersed beneath the water three times. The ceremony of Chrismation, anointing the body with oil, is carried out immediately afterward to complete the baptism. Chrism is a mixture of olive oil and balsam, together with other ingredients, that is used in anointing at Ordination as well as Baptism and Confirmation. Finally, the baby is dressed in new clothes to symbolize the eternal life ahead, which has just been received through Baptism.

4.3
BELIEVER'S BAPTISM

The Baptist Church as well as some other Protestant Churches argue strenuously that there is only one form of Baptism described in the New Testament - adult Believer's Baptism. Members of these Churches believe that they should follow the example of Jesus and wait until they are adults.

THEY POINT OUT THAT:

1. Jesus was baptized by John the Baptist in the Jordan River - as an adult. By offering himself for baptism, Jesus was identifying himself with those men and women who were confessing their sins and receiving forgiveness at John's hands.

2. Peter, on the Day of Pentecost, told his converts to: "...turn away from your sins and be baptized in the name of Jesus Christ, so that your sins will be forgiven; and you will receive God's gift, the Holy Spirit"

Romans 6.4

"By our baptism, then, we were buried with him and shared his death, in order that, just as Christ was raised from death by the glorious power of the Father, so also we might live a new life."

[Acts 2.38]. In the preaching of the early Christians these four elements - repentance, baptism, forgiveness, and receiving the Holy Spirit - were often linked.

3. Paul used the symbolism of Believer's Baptism to describe what had happened to those beginning the Christian life.

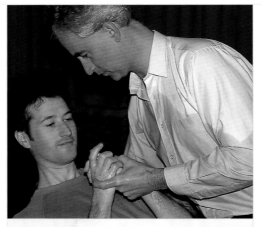

Above: Many Christians do not agree with Infant Baptism because in the Bible only adults were baptized.

Although he sometimes needed to remind his readers of the significance of baptism he took it for granted that it was regularly performed. This was the reason why he was able to explain the symbolic significance of the ritual.

BELIEVER'S BAPTISM

When it comes to being baptized many Christians want to follow the example of Jesus as closely as possible. To this end some actually travel to the Jordan River but others settle for any stream, river, lake, or sea nearby. The majority, though, are baptized in their local Baptist Church where a pool [baptistery] is sunk into the ground at the front of the building. Although such baptisms were carried out in the early Church only at Easter and Whitsun (the festival celebrating the giving of the Holy Spirit) they can now be performed at any time. The custom of wearing white for the service - the color of purity - largely remains.

The service is performed in front of the whole church and this is important. Each person to be baptized makes a personal statement of their own faith in Christ, describing how they became a Christian and what Christ means to them. Three important symbolic acts then take place:

1. They go down into the pool where the minister, or church leader, waits for them. By going down into the pool the person shows that they are leaving their old sinful life firmly behind them.

2. Their body is immersed totally beneath the water by the minister. This symbolizes the "dying with Christ" which lies at the heart of Believer's Baptism. The split second that they are beneath the water shows that the believer is "buried with Christ."

Mark 1.9-10

"Not long afterwards Jesus came from Nazareth in the province of Galilee and was baptized by John in the Jordan. As soon as Jesus came up out of the water, he saw heaven opening and the Spirit coming down on him like a dove. And a voice came from heaven: 'You are my own dear Son. I am pleased with you.'"

RIGHT: *The inspiration for Christian baptism is the baptism of Jesus.*

3. They come up out of the water, leaving the pool by different steps to show that the person now shares "the resurrection life" of Christ. Just as Jesus rose to enjoy eternal life with God so the person baptized is now sharing in that new life as well.

No spiritual change takes place as a result of Believer's Baptism. The service is full of symbolism to indicate those changes that have already taken place in the person's life - or are continuing to do so. A very strong parallel is drawn with the death, burial, and resurrection of Jesus since baptism is the means by which each believer can share in those events.

The next step is for the believer to be received into full and active membership of the local church. This takes place at the first Lord's Supper after baptism when the person is given "the right hand of fellowship" by the minister and welcomed as a full member of the Church. He or she is now expected to play a part in the work of the Church by proclaiming the Christian Gospel to all those around.

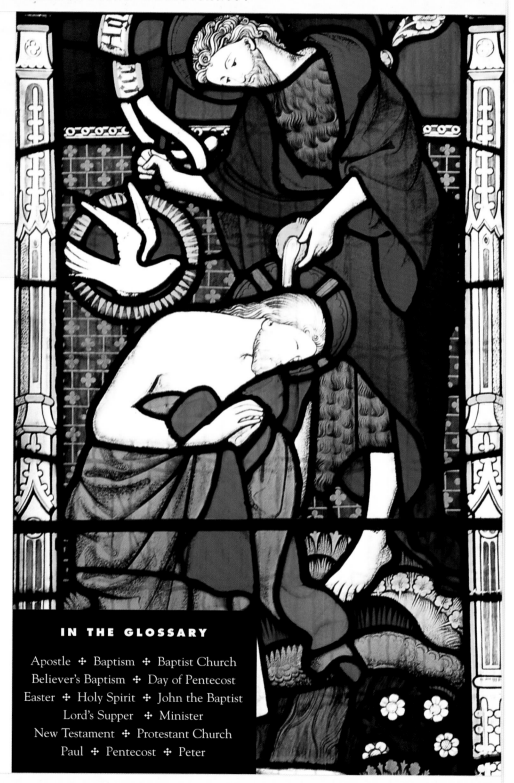

IN THE GLOSSARY

Apostle ✛ Baptism ✛ Baptist Church
Believer's Baptism ✛ Day of Pentecost
Easter ✛ Holy Spirit ✛ John the Baptist
Lord's Supper ✛ Minister
New Testament ✛ Protestant Church
Paul ✛ Pentecost ✛ Peter

4.4
CHURCH MEMBERSHIP

During the New Testament period the rituals of baptism and "the laying-on of hands" to bestow the gift of the Holy Spirit were carried out at the same time on adult converts. As the Church later began to accept Infant Baptism, Confirmation was reserved as a sacrament to be performed when a child grew up. The Orthodox Church, though, still retains the old practice of combining Baptism and Confirmation [Chrismation] in the same service.

I n the Anglican tradition, and some parts of the Protestant tradition as well, the emphasis is placed on believers affirming their own religious faith at Confirmation and making their own the very promises that others made for them when they were baptized. In the Roman Catholic Church, Confirmation, together with the taking of Holy Communion, makes the spiritual life begun at Baptism possible. As the person makes a public commitment to Jesus so they are believed

St. Ambrose

"Recall then that you have received the spiritual seal, the spirit of wisdom and understanding, the spirit of right judgment and courage, the spirit of knowledge and reverence, the spirit of Holy fear in God's presence. Guard what you have received. God the Father has marked you with his sign; Christ the Lord has confirmed you and placed his pledge, the Spirit, in your hearts."

to receive the Holy Spirit in a special way. In both Anglican and Catholic traditions Confirmation often takes place in the early teenage years, although it can take place later for someone who has been converted to the faith.

THE CONFIRMATION SERVICE

This service is always performed by a bishop in episcopal Churches, since he or she, alone, has been authorized to transmit God's blessing through the laying-on of hands. During the service the same questions asked of parents and godparents at Baptism are repeated, but this time the person can answer for him- or herself, therefore taking responsibility for their own spiritual welfare.

When the questions have been answered the bishop lays his hands on the head of each candidate. This practice goes back to the earliest days of the Christian faith. Then, as now, it is the means by which the Holy Spirit is passed on. Two further features of the service in a Roman Catholic Church are worth noting:

1. THE CANDIDATES ARE ANOINTED WITH OIL [chrism]. From earliest times oil was rubbed into wounds to help them to heal. Here, though, it is the healing of the soul rather than the body that is being symbolized.

2. THE BISHOP LIGHTLY SLAPS THE FACE OF EACH CANDIDATE WITH TWO FINGERS. This symbolic gesture highlights the suffering and contempt that each new Christian may have to suffer. The service represents a new beginning - with all the peace of mind that comes from having one's sins forgiven.

LEFT: At Confirmation the bishop lays his hands upon the person's head.

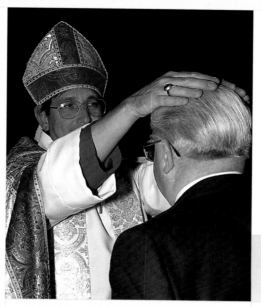

LEFT: Confirmation is an important service in many Churches. It marks the beginning of a person's Christian commitment.

✣ ✣ ✣

THE METHODIST CHURCH'S TICKET OF MEMBERSHIP

✣ ✣ ✣

All those who confess Jesus Christ as Lord and Savior and accept the obligation to serve him in the life of the Church and the world are welcome as full members of the Methodist Church.

In the Church: Members are committed to worship, Holy Communion, fellowship and service, prayer and Bible study, and responsible giving.

In the world: Members are committed to the working out of their faith in daily life, the offering of personal service in the community, the Christian use of their resources, and the support of the Church in its total world mission.

THE METHODIST CHURCH

In the Methodist Church a person who has been baptized becomes a Church member when the hands of the minister are placed on their head. Each year, following this, Methodists sign a ticket of membership which commits them to several responsibilities within the Church. This covenant is renewed at the annual Covenant service held on the first Sunday of each new year.

Catechism of the Catholic Church

"If a Christian is in danger of death, any priest should give him Confirmation. Indeed the Church desires that none of her children, even the youngest, should depart this world without having been perfected by the Holy Spirit with the gift of Christ's fullness."

IN THE GLOSSARY

Anglican Church ✣ Baptism
Baptist Church ✣ Bishop ✣ Chrism
Confirmation ✣ Episcopacy
Holy Communion ✣ Holy Spirit
Infant Baptism ✣ Lord's Supper
Methodist Church ✣ Minister
New Testament ✣ Orthodox Church
Protestant ✣ Roman Catholic Church
Sacrament

4.5
HOLY COMMUNION

For the vast majority of Christians, Holy Communion, or the Eucharist, is the most important act of worship. "Holy Communion" means "holy sharing" and refers to the sharing within the Christian community of the bread and wine with each other - and with God.

IN THE BEGINNING

It is the clear link between Holy Communion and the life and ministry of Jesus that gives the service its unique place in the Church's worship. From the beginning of the early Church, Christians met together to "break bread" because they were convinced that Jesus had told them to do so - a belief underlined by the fact that all four Gospels and one Epistle report his words. We are told that, on the night on which he was betrayed, Jesus took a loaf of bread, broke it, and gave a piece to each of his disciples with the words:

"Take and eat it. This is my body" [Matthew 26.26].

Moments later he took a goblet of wine and passed it around among his friends, saying to them:

"Drink it, all of you…this is my blood, which seals God's covenant, my blood poured out for many for the forgiveness of sins" [Matthew 26.27,28].

These words form the basis of the modern service of Holy Communion.

DIFFERENT NAMES

Throughout their long history the Churches have disagreed about the precise

1 Corinthians 11.23-26

"… on the night he was betrayed, [Jesus] took a piece of bread, gave thanks to God, broke it and said, 'This is my body, which is for you. Do this in memory of me.' In the same way, after the supper he took the cup and said, 'This cup is God's new covenant, sealed with my blood. Whenever you drink it, do so in memory of me.'"

ABOVE: *Holy Communion is one of only two symbols that can be traced directly back to Jesus himself.*

meaning of Holy Communion. These differences are reflected in the various names that the service carries:

a. In the Roman Catholic Church it is called "the Mass," probably from the last words of the old Latin service - Ita Missa Est ["Go it is finished"].

b. In Orthodox Churches the service is called "the Divine Liturgy." The "liturgy" is an order of service that has been hallowed by time, and the Divine Liturgy goes back, in form, to St. John Chrysostom [347-407].

c. For Anglicans the service is mainly called "the Eucharist" ["thanksgiving"] or Holy Communion.

d. In Protestant Churches two terms are traditionally used - "the Breaking of Bread" [as Jesus broke bread with his disciples at the Last Supper] or "the Lord's Supper" [a phrase taken from Paul].

THE MEANING

In their understanding of the meaning of the service of Holy Communion there is a fundamental difference between Roman Catholic and Orthodox believers on the one hand and Protestants [Anglicans] on the other:

+ Protestants believe that Holy Communion is no more than an act of remembrance. By eating the bread and drinking the wine each worshiper is able to come to a deeper understanding of the death of Christ. The bread and wine remain as symbols that are able to point to that deeper understanding; they have no other significance for Protestants.
+ Anglicans/Episcopalians look upon the bread and wine in Holy Communion as the transmitters of spiritual blessing. For them, something real and very spiritual happens during Holy Communion, although the elements remain as bread and wine.
+ The Roman Catholic and Orthodox Churches believe that Christ is

ABOVE: As it does in all the other sacraments, the Church makes use of basic symbols in the service of Holy Communion. The bread symbolizes the body of Jesus Christ and the wine, the blood of Jesus Christ.

"really" present in the bread [the host] and the wine. This transformation happens once the bread and wine have been "consecrated" to God by the priest during the Mass or Divine Liturgy. Because the bread and wine become the actual body and blood of Jesus Christ [transubstantiation], the service becomes a reenactment of the death of Jesus on the cross in which his body and blood are once again offered as a sacrifice to God.

The Catechism of the Catholic Church, 1327

"In brief, the Eucharist is the sum and summary of our faith: Our way of thinking is attuned to the Eucharist and the Eucharist in turn confirms our way of thinking."

IN THE GLOSSARY

Anglican Church ✛ Breaking of Bread
Divine Liturgy ✛ Epistle ✛ Eucharist
Gospel ✛ Holy Communion ✛ Host
Last Supper ✛ Lord's Supper
Mass ✛ Orthodox Church
Protestant Church
Quakers ✛ Reformation
Roman Catholic Church
Salvation Army ✛ Transubstantiation

4.6
THE EUCHARIST

In the Anglican/Episcopal Church the service of Holy Communion is often called the Eucharist [thanksgiving]. The meaning and emphasis of this service has changed considerably over the centuries. In the old Book of Common Prayer [1662] two aspects of the service were emphasized:

a. The sufferings of Christ that led up to his death on the cross.

b. The humble and penitent approach of the worshiper as he or she came forward to receive the sacrament.

The Alternative Service Book, published in 1980, preferred to emphasize the importance of God's creation and the resurrection of Jesus from the dead.

The frequency with which the Eucharist is celebrated is some guide to the importance that a particular Anglican or Episcopal church attaches to this sacrament. In Anglo-Catholic churches, for instance, the Eucharist is firmly placed at the center of all worship and is celebrated several times a week, if not daily. In other churches the norm is for the Eucharist to be celebrated once each Sunday and on one other occasion during the week. In addition, celebrations of the Eucharist are often held on special Church festivals such as Ascension Day, and these celebrations are linked to the special theme of the day.

LEFT: Most Protestant Churches make use of individual cups but in the Anglican Church a communal goblet is used. This emphasizes the communal aspect of the Eucharistic meal.

Alternative Service Book
The Eucharist

Instead of recreating the sacrifice of Christ on the cross, as the Roman Catholic Mass does, the Anglican Eucharist service has now become a community meal in which everyone shares. This "sharing" aspect is stressed by the giving of the "Peace" just before the bread and wine are shared among the people. At this moment in the service the people shake hands, hug, or kiss while passing on the words *"The Peace of the Lord be with you"* to each other

Once the priest has blessed the bread and wine he says to all the communicants:

"Draw near and receive the body of our Lord Jesus Christ, which was given for you, and his blood, which was shed for you. Take this in remembrance that Christ died for you, and feed on him in your hearts by faith with thanksgiving."

As they receive the bread the priest says to each person:
"The body of Christ"
and as he hands them the wine he says:
"The blood of Christ"
and they reply each time:
"Amen [so be it]."

IN THE GLOSSARY

Alternative Service Book
Anglican Church ✛ Ascension Day
Book of Common Prayer ✛ Eucharist
Evangelical ✛ Holy Communion
Low Church ✛ Mass ✛ Peace
Roman Catholic Church
Sacrament ✛ Sunday

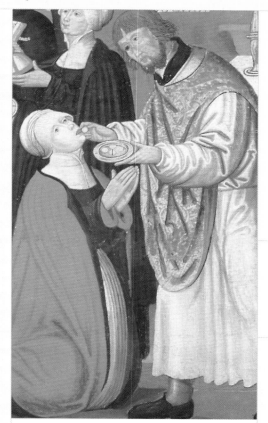

THE MEANING OF THE EUCHARIST

The Anglican Church is a "Broad Church." This means that it has always included many different beliefs and points of view among its members. In Anglo-Catholic congregations the words of the Eucharist are interpreted along Roman Catholic lines with a change taking place in the bread and wine as they become the actual body and blood of Christ. Low Church [Evangelical] Anglicans, however, share the Protestant belief that the Eucharist is a "commemoration" of the Last Supper with the symbols remaining just what they are. For the majority, though, the Eucharist is the time when God blesses the members of the congregation in a way that does not happen in any other service.

✛ ✛ ✛
OPENING COLLECT
✛ ✛ ✛

Almighty God, unto whom all hearts be open, all desires known, and from whom no secrets are hid, cleanse the thoughts of our hearts by the inspiration of thy Holy Spirit, that we may perfectly love thee, and worthily magnify thy holy name; through Christ, our Lord. Amen

LEFT: *The various Anglican Churches have their own specific interpretation of the Eucharist service.*

The Eucharistic Prayer in the Anglican Church

This prayer is prayed by the priest in the Alternative Service Book Eucharist:
"...Who in the same night that he was betrayed;
took bread and gave you thanks;
he broke it and gave to his disciples, saying:
'Take, eat; this is my body which is given for you,
do this in remembrance of me.'
In the same way, after supper he took the cup and gave thanks;
he gave it to them, saying:
'Drink this, all of you;
this is the blood of my new covenant, which is shed for you, and for many, for the forgiveness of sin.
Do this, as often as you drink it, in remembrance of me.'"

4.7
THE MASS

For most Roman Catholics going to Mass and receiving the elements of bread and wine are at the center of their lives as Christians. The Mass is celebrated daily in every Catholic church, and Catholics are obliged to attend the service regularly as well as on holy days of obligation. The service is a weekly renewal of faith as people listen to the Word of God from the Bible readings, pray together, and receive the Eucharistic elements.

THE FORGIVENESS OF SINS

Catholics believe that in order to participate fully in the Mass they must be cleansed from their sins. A Catholic who has committed a serious sin can receive absolution only through confession, but everyone present at Mass receives forgiveness for lesser [venial] sins through the "penitential rite" at the beginning of the service. All Catholics make the sign of the cross with holy water as they enter the Church as a way of preparing themselves for the service.

Preface to the
Holy Eucharist [Mass]

"He [Christ] is the true and eternal priest who establishes this unending sacrifice. He offered himself as a victim for our deliverance and taught us to make this offering in his memory. As we eat his body which he gave for us, we grow in strength. As we drink his blood which is poured out for us, we are washed clean."

THE LITURGY OF THE MASS

a. THE LITURGY OF THE WORD. As the Mass opens, the people are invited to repent of their sins and seek forgiveness from God. This forgiveness is pronounced on the people by the priest. Three passages from the Bible - the Old Testament, the Gospels, and the Epistles - preface the sermon preached by the priest. The readings are taken from a Lectionary, which is based on a three-year cycle to cover the four Gospels. The readings are followed by a sermon [homily] based on one of the passages, the recitation of the Nicene Creed, and prayers of intercession seeking the blessing of God on the Church and on the world.

b. THE LITURGY OF THE EUCHARIST. The people then bring forward their gifts of money, bread, and wine to the altar, symbolizing the belief that the Mass is a sacrifice of the people as well as that of Jesus. After the priest has washed his hands he says the Eucharistic prayer, which brings together the needs of the people with the sacrifice of Christ that is

The Eucharistic Prayer.
The Sunday Missal

"Almighty God, we pray that your angel may take this sacrifice to your altar in heaven. Then as we receive from this altar the sacred body and blood of your Son, let us be filled with every grace and blessing."

about to be renewed in the Mass. The prayer of consecration then follows before the priest repeats the words of Jesus that were spoken at the Last Supper. At this point the bread and wine are changed into the actual body and blood of Christ, with a bell being rung to indicate this. The priest then continues with the Eucharistic prayer.

The people join together in the Lord's Prayer [the "Our Father"] to pray for their daily food and forgiveness. Before sharing Holy Communion together they give each other the sign of peace as an open demonstration of their love for one another. The priest then takes Holy

RIGHT: The thin, round wafer consecrated by the priest during the Roman Catholic Holy Communion service is called the "host" [sacrifice, victim].

Communion and distributes it among the people. Any remaining hosts are placed back in the tabernacle.

Finally, everyone is sent out into the world to help their neighbor, especially if that neighbor is in need. By serving others they are not only helping those in need but serving God as well. They are also strengthening their own spiritual lives, something they have already done by sharing the Mass together. The priest dismisses members of the congregation with the following words: "Go in peace to love and serve the Lord."

The Catechism of the Catholic Church says:

In the Eucharist Christ gives us the very body which he gave up for us on the cross, the very blood which he "poured out for many for the forgiveness of sins." The Mass is so important for all Catholics because it is the means by which their spiritual lives are renewed day by day. Not only does the Mass unite Catholics with Jesus Christ but it also unites them with each other.

4.8

THE DIVINE LITURGY

The liturgy ["the people's work of thanksgiving"] is any service of worship that follows a form laid down, and hallowed, by tradition. In the Orthodox Church the term is applied in a specific sense to the Divine Liturgy, which is the service of Holy Communion. Orthodox Christians believe that the liturgy goes back to the earliest days of Christianity when it was the Church's blessing of bread and wine. The Divine Liturgy is divided into two clear parts - the Liturgy of the Word and the Liturgy of the Faithful.

THE LITURGY OF THE WORD

This part of the service includes prayers, Bible readings, and a sermon and has its equivalent in both the Anglican/ Episcopalian Communion service and the Catholic Mass. The climax to the Liturgy of the Word comes when the priest, carrying the Book of the Gospels high above his head, comes through the Royal Doors in the middle of the iconostasis (the screen at the front of the church). Surrounded by attendants carrying candles, the priest reads a passage from the Gospels before returning through the iconostasis back to the High Altar.

THE LITURGY OF THE FAITHFUL

Most of the Liturgy of the Faithful is conducted behind the iconostasis although the congregation can see enough of the service to follow what is happening. The iconostasis has an important

RIGHT: During the Divine Liturgy, a priest of the Orthodox Church carries the Book of Gospels through the Royal Doors of the iconostasis.

symbolic significance in the Orthodox liturgy; it indicates the chasm that must exist between a holy God and sinful human beings. This gulf is so great that only the priest, through his ordination to the priesthood, is allowed to bridge it and enter directly into God's presence, which is symbolically represented by the High Altar. The people are allowed to glimpse that presence from a distance but they are not allowed to draw close.

The Liturgy of the Faithful is the central part of Holy Communion. It begins with the preparation of the bread and wine for communion. The priest stands at the altar while he is doing this, repeating short prayers while the Royal Doors are closed. This symbolizes the holiness of the death of Jesus and the elements, bread and wine, by which it is represented to the people. The people then respond with the words:

"Kyrie eleison" [Lord have mercy].

A Psalm and the Little Litany are sung, with the people again responding:

"Kyrie eleison."

The Beatitudes are read before the Gospel is carried above the heads of the people as they sing three times:

"Holy God, holy and mighty, holy and immortal, have mercy on us."

The Grand Entrance follows, as servers process with candles and incense, and the priest carries the bread and wine. The people bow as the procession passes by The Royal Doors are opened, allowing the priests to pass through into the sanctuary. The bread and wine are laid on the Holy Table - the altar. The people greet one another with the kiss of peace before reciting the Nicene Creed. In the prayers

that follow, the story of the Last Supper is retold before everyone joins in the Lord's Prayer. Finally the priest raises the bread and breaks it - a part of the service called the "elevation." The choir sings and bells are rung.

The priest then stands in front of the Royal Doors and those who are receiving Communion come forward and kneel before the priest. Each person receives a piece of bread dipped in wine and placed at the back of the throat on a silver spoon. After taking Communion everyone comes up to kiss the cross that the priest is

The Nicene Creed

*"We believe in one God, the Father,
the almighty, maker of heaven and earth,
of all that is seen and unseen.
We believe in one Lord, Jesus Christ,
the only Son of God, eternally begotten
of the Father, God from God,
Light from Light, true God from true
God, begotten, not made, of one Being
with the father. Through him all things
were made. For us men and our
salvation he came down from heaven;
by the power of the Holy Spirit he
became incarnate of the Virgin Mary and
was made man. For our sake he was
crucified under Pontius Pilate;
he suffered death and was buried.
On the third day he rose again according
to the Scriptures; he ascended into
heaven and is seated on the right hand
of the Father. He will come in glory…
We believe in the Holy Spirit…
We believe in one holy catholic and
apostolic church…We look for the
resurrection from the dead…Amen."*

holding, and a small piece of bread is shared together as a sign of fellowship and love - just as the early Christians shared their meals together.

UNDERSTANDING THE DIVINE LITURGY

The Divine Liturgy is service that appeals to all the senses, with the ornate vestments worn by the clergy, the clouds of incense that fill the air, and the beautiful music. This beauty is a very important element in the meaning of the Divine Liturgy. The icons [religious paintings], which cover the iconostasis and are found elsewhere in the church, provide the key to understanding the significance of the service. Made according to holy traditions that go back centuries, the icons radiate the glory of the subjects painted on them - whether it is Jesus, Mary, or one of the saints. Because of this they are "peep-holes into eternity" as well as being the means of bringing worshipers into contact with eternal matters. Through experiencing the Divine Liturgy the people are able to imagine what life is like in heaven. In particular, it opens up to them a glimpse of God.

IN THE GLOSSARY

Altar ✣ Anglican Church
Beatitudes ✣ Divine Liturgy
Gospels ✣ Holy Communion ✣ Icon
Iconostasis ✣ Last Supper ✣ Liturgy
Lord's Prayer ✣ Mary ✣ Mass
Nicene Creed ✣ Ordination
Orthodox Church ✣ Priest ✣ Psalm
Roman Catholic Church
Royal Doors ✣ Saint ✣ Sermon

4.9
THE LORD'S SUPPER
THE BREAKING OF BREAD

Protestants try to keep their worship and devotions as close to the Bible as possible. They have two favorite terms for Holy Communion, the service in which they remember and draw strength from the death of Jesus. The first, "the Breaking of Bread," is a direct quotation from the New Testament. The second, "the Lord's Supper," was Paul's own preferred description of the fellowship meal shared by all Christian believers.

Clearly the early Christians often met together to share an ordinary meal. Quite apart from being an act of worship this meal also served a very practical purpose - to feed those who were hungry and needy in the early Christian community. It was also a symbol. By bringing together the wealthy and the needy it was a practical expression of the unity and practicality of Christian fellowship. This time of sharing and fellowship, though, was always enjoyed in the light of Christ's expected return to earth.

RIGHT: The Gospel story of the Last Supper provided the basis for Church ritual and prayers during Holy Communion.

Mark 14.22-24

"While they were eating, Jesus took a piece of bread, gave a prayer of thanks, broke it, and gave it to his disciples, 'Take it,' he said, 'this is my body.' Then he took a cup, gave thanks to God, and handed it to them; and they all drank from it. Jesus said, 'This is my blood which is poured out for many, my blood which seals God's covenant.'"

Acts 20.7

"On the first day of the week we came together to break bread…"
[New International Version translation]

RIGHT: Jesus with his Apostles at the Last Supper. Protestants, especially Baptists, try to fashion the Lord's Supper, also known as the Breaking of Bread, to resemble as closely as possible the last meal that Jesus shared with his Apostles.

THE LORD'S SUPPER

In most Protestant churches the Lord's Supper is celebrated twice a month - after the morning and evening services. The people begin by confessing their sins to God before listening to a passage from the Bible. This passage might describe the last meal that Jesus ate with his Apostles [Luke 22.7-13] or Paul's description of the meal [1 Corinthians 11.17-34]. The minister

1 Corinthians 11.33

"So then, my brothers and sisters, when you gather together to eat the Lord's Supper, wait for one another."

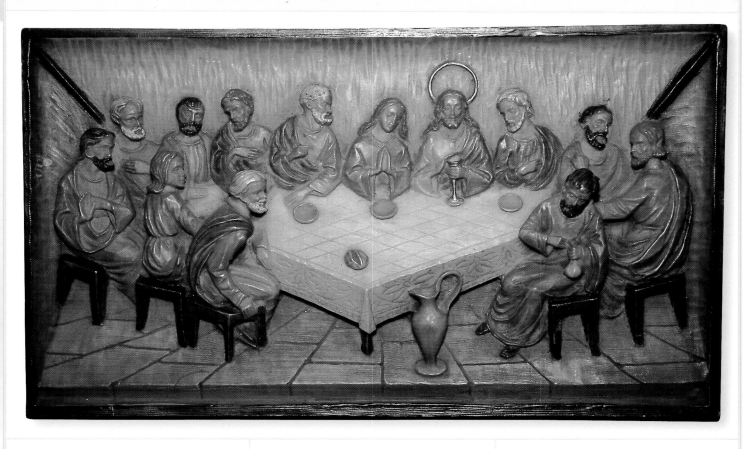

spends a short time explaining the meaning of the service and a collection is taken up for the needy in the church. Following this, the bread and wine are placed on the Communion table [there being no altar in a Protestant church] or a cloth covering the bread and wine on the table is removed. The bread and wine are consecrated to God as the minister, or leader, reads the words spoken by Jesus at the Last Supper.

In Methodist churches the people kneel at the rail at the front of the church to receive the bread and wine, but in most Protestant churches they remain in their seats while a loaf of bread is passed around. Each person takes the bread and eats it at once to symbolize the Protestant belief that each person must answer spiritually to God for him- or herself. However, the people do not drink the tiny glass of wine until everyone has received one. Then they drink the wine together to symbolize the importance of the unity of Christian fellowship.

IN THE GLOSSARY

Bible ✛ Breaking of Bread
Holy Communion ✛ Last Supper
Lord's Supper ✛ Minister
New Testament
Paul ✛ Protestant
Reformation ✛ Transubstantiation

Protestants do not believe that anything happens to the bread and wine during Communion. The Catholic belief in transubstantiation [that the bread and wine become the actual body and blood of Jesus] was emphatically rejected at the Protestant Reformation. For Protestants, the bread and wine simply act as important pointers and symbols of much deeper spiritual realities. As they are taken and consumed they stimulate the worshiper to meditate and reflect on the death and resurrection of Jesus. This is why the minister advises members of the congregation as they take the bread and wine to:

"Feed on him [Jesus Christ] in your hearts by faith."

4.10
MARRIAGE

In the Roman Catholic and Orthodox Churches marriage is a sacrament - a special channel along which the blessing of God flows. Anglican and Protestant Churches do not see marriage as a sacrament but they teach that it is a special binding agreement made in the presence of God between a man and a woman who love each other. This love is, as Paul teaches, a reflection of the love that exists between Christ and the Church.

Although wedding services vary, three common themes unite those that are performed in a church. These services emphasize that:

a. THE WEDDING TAKES PLACE IN THE SIGHT OF GOD - and in the presence of human witnesses. God is the most

Ephesians 5.31-33

"As the Scripture says, 'For this reason a man will leave his father and mother and unite with his wife, and the two will become one.' There is a deep secret truth in this scripture, which I understand as applying to Christ and the Church. But it also applies to you: every husband must love his wife as himself, and every wife must respect her husband."

important witness to the new marriage and it is this element, more than any other, that distinguishes a church wedding from those that take place elsewhere.

b. THE MARRIAGE IS A LIFELONG COMMITMENT between the two people although every Church, except for the Roman Catholic, has felt it necessary to come to terms with divorce. In all church weddings, however, the man and woman promise to be faithful to each other until death separates them.

c. CHILDREN. Every marriage can expect to be blessed with the gift of children although, in truth, many are not. More and more couples are choosing not to have children. It is also a sad fact that one in ten couples cannot conceive a child.

THE WEDDING SERVICE

In Anglican/Episcopal Churches the priest provides three reasons for marriage:

a. SO THAT TWO PEOPLE CAN LOVE AND CARE FOR ONE ANOTHER. Marriage is the best possible relationship in which this can take place.

b. TO PROVIDE THE MOST LOVING AND SECURE ENVIRONMENT in which sexual intercourse can be enjoyed.

c. TO PROVIDE A LOVING AND STABLE HOME ENVIRONMENT into which children can be born and grow up.

During the service the couple promise to: "love, comfort, honor, and protect each other in sickness and health as long as they both shall live."

The man places a ring on the third finger of the bride's left hand [they may exchange rings instead] saying:

RIGHT: Having children, and providing a stable, loving home for them, is one of the reasons for marriage.

LEFT: In a Christian marriage the relationship is blessed by God and the ceremony is performed in front of witnesses.

Preface to Wedding Mass in Roman Catholic Missal

"The love of man and woman is made holy in the Sacrament of Marriage, and becomes the mirror of your everlasting love."

IN THE GLOSSARY

Anglican Church ✦ Episcopal Church
Missal ✦ Nonconformist Church
Nuptial Mass ✦ Orthodox Church
Paul ✦ Roman Catholic Church
Sacrament

Nuptial Mass. There is a basic difference between marriage and the other sacraments. In the other sacraments the priest bestows the blessing on the people but in marriage the couple uniquely bestow the sacrament, and its blessings, on each other. They symbolize this by offering each other the bread and wine at the end of the special Nuptial Mass.

There is a rather beautiful variation in the Orthodox Church wedding service. The priest crowns the couple with "wreaths" indicating that they will become king and queen over their own small kingdom - the house that they will be setting up together.

To symbolize this unity the couple share a glass of wine and walk three times, hand in hand, around a table in the center of the church.

"I give you this ring as a sign of our marriage. With my body I honor you, all that I am I give to you, and all that I have I share with you within the love of God."

In all Churches the ring, a perfect and unbroken circle, is a symbol of that love that, if genuine, will last for eternity. The priest pronounces the couple husband and wife with the words:

"That which God has joined together, let no man divide."

When a marriage takes place between two Roman Catholics, the wedding service is finished with the celebration of a

4.11

ORDINATION, PENANCE, AND ANOINTING

In the Roman Catholic Church a man who is ordained as a deacon takes a vow of perpetual celibacy. Twelve months later, as he sits among the people that he serves, he is ordained to the priesthood. The bishop confirms that the Church has called him to the priesthood. The deacon places his hands between those of the bishop as the two of them agree to work together to further Christ's Gospel. The bishop invites the congregation to pray for the priest as he prostrates himself, face downward, on the floor.

As the moment of ordination approaches the candidate kneels before the bishop, who lays his hands on his head. The bishop is showing that the person has received the gift of the Holy Spirit which will make him a priest. The priest is ordained when the bishop says the prayer of consecration. The new priest puts on the vestments of priesthood - the stole and the chasuble. His hands are anointed with oil before he is presented to the people, and the bishop hands him the elements of bread and wine. The most important part of his future ministry will be to dispense the Eucharist as well as to baptize babies, marry his parishioners, and bury the dead. He will also be expected to set the members of his congregation a

RIGHT: Priest hearing confession.
Since Vatican II the nature of the relationship between the priest and the penitent has changed.

clear example by the quality of his spiritual life. He can only do this through God's strength, so his ordination ends with his offer of the Peace to the bishop and other priests in the congregation.

Once ordained the priest will be able to offer the sacraments to members of his congregation. These include the following:
a. PENANCE. A person becomes a member of the Catholic community through Baptism and Confirmation. But this is only

The Perfect Church Leader - Titus 1.6-9

"Since a church leader is in charge of God's work, he should be blameless. He must not be arrogant or short-tempered, or a drunkard or violent or greedy for money. He must be hospitable and love what is good. He must be self-controlled, upright, holy, and disciplined. He must hold firmly to the message which can be trusted and which agrees with the doctrine."

the beginning of a long process of growth, since human beings are sinful. Christians are called by God to be perfect - and yet are increasingly aware of their imperfections. To help them the Catholic Church offers the sacrament of Penance and Reconciliation [confession]. Although this sacrament has been a part of the Church's worship for centuries it was given a new focus by the Second Vatican Council [1962-65]. Since the 17th century, when the "confessional box" was introduced to ensure privacy, the emphasis was upon confessing sin and receiving

absolution from the priest. After Vatican II, however, reconciliation became a face-to-face conversation in which counseling and more direct help was offered. Although the priest now knows the identity of the person confessing he is still bound by the "seal of confession" to absolute secrecy.

When the person has confessed, the priest offers a few words of encouragement and advice before suggesting a simple penance, such as the saying of a few prayers, so that people can show God that they are sorry for their sins. Forgiveness is available only to those who show that they are genuinely repentant for their past actions and determined to change their lives in the future. After this happens, the priest can use the ministry of forgiveness entrusted to him at ordination and can assure the person that he or she is forgiven by God. The priest then makes the sign of the cross as he says:

"I absolve you from your sins in the name of the Father, and of the Son, and of the Holy Spirit."

Through the sacrament of Reconciliation the baptismal relationship between God and the person is restored.
b. ANOINTING THE SICK. In 1972 Pope Paul VI introduced the new rite of anointing the sick. This is intended to assure people who are ill that they are not alone in their suffering and to celebrate with them the privilege of sharing in the sufferings of Christ. The sick person, and others present, are sprinkled with holy water to remind them that they began to follow Jesus when they were baptized. Hands are laid on the person's head as the priest prays for a healing. Then the head

James 5.14,15

"Are any of you ill? You should send for the Church elders, who will pray for them and rub olive oil on them in the name of the Lord. This prayer made in faith will heal the sick; the Lord will restore them to health, and the sins they have commited will be forgiven."

and hands are anointed with consecrated oil. The sick are usually given the bread and wine of Holy Communion since this unites them with Christ in a special way. If they are dying, and this might be their last Communion [viaticum] then they are reminded of their baptismal promises and assured that they are traveling to their Father in heaven.

IN THE GLOSSARY

Absolution ✤ Baptism ✤ Bishop
Celibacy ✤ Confirmation ✤ Deacon
Eucharist ✤ Holy Communion
Holy Spirit ✤ Ordination ✤ Peace
Penance ✤ Priest ✤ Roman Catholic
Church ✤ Viaticum

4.12
DEATH

The Christian Church has always held clearly defined beliefs about life after death and these are reflected in the funeral services held across the different denominations. Underlying all other beliefs is the Christian conviction that death is not the end and that the soul [the spiritual part of each person] survives death. Furthermore, at the end of time the body will be resurrected to share in Christ's own victory over death.

ORTHODOX FUNERALS

The Orthodox Church believes that there is no difference between the living and dead. Just as we pray for those who are living so we must pray for those who have died. These prayers begin as soon as death

The Kontakion - a Greek Orthodox funeral prayer

"Give rest, O Christ, to all thy servants with thy saints. Where sorrow and pain are no more, neither sighing but life everlasting. Thou only art immortal, the creator and maker of man, And we are mortal born of earth, and unto earth will we return, all we go down to the dust."

takes place. The body is washed, dressed in new clothes, and placed in an open coffin. A strip of material containing icons of John the Baptist, Mary, and Jesus is placed across the forehead of the corpse and an icon placed in the hand. The body is then covered with a linen cloth to symbolize the protection that Christ offers everyone, whether they are dead or alive. The coffin lid is closed for the last time when the service is over.

Death is God's punishment for sin, so is a tragedy. Yet even in great grief and bereavement there is hope for the believer. This hope is expressed in the Orthodox funeral by the burning candles and the incense that is freely wafted over the coffin. The Bible readings encourage everyone to look forward to the future time when Christ will return to the earth and everyone will be raised from the dead.

PROTESTANT AND ROMAN CATHOLIC FUNERALS

In a Roman Catholic service the coffin is taken to the church on the night before the funeral so that prayers can be said for the soul of the deceased. Catholics believe that each soul spends some time in purgatory - a place located between heaven and hell - after death. The amount of time they finally spend there can be directly affected by the prayers of those on earth, so praying for the dead is an important Catholic tradition.

For the service the Roman Catholic priest wears white robes, which is the color traditionally associated with life after

Protestant funeral prayer from the United Reformed Church

"For as much as it hath pleased Almighty God of His great mercy to take unto himself the soul of our dear brother/sister departed, we therefore commit his/her body to the ground; earth to earth, ashes to ashes, dust to dust; in sure and certain hope of resurrection to everlasting life through our Lord Jesus Christ."

death and the resurrection of the body. These two themes are central in the funeral service. As the priest meets the coffin at the door and sprinkles it with holy water he repeats the words from John's Gospel:

"I am the Resurrection and the Life. Those who believe in me will live, even though they die; and all those who live and believe in me will never die" [11.25]

The service then takes the form of a Requiem Mass during which the prayer is offered:

"Eternal rest grant unto them, O Lord, and let light perpetual rest on them."

The same themes of purgatory and the eternal rest of the soul are also stressed in the Anglo-Catholic Church. Most Protestants, however, do not believe in purgatory although they do strongly believe in life after death. In Protestant funeral services, when a person has died his or her soul is committed to God's safe keeping through hymns, prayers, Bible readings, and a short eulogy [a sermon of praise] about the dead person. The Bible readings and prayers reflect the Protestant view that once a person has died their soul is with God in heaven. Everyone then looks forward to the end of time when all Christian believers will receive a "new body" similar to the one that Christ had when he returned from the dead.

The service is followed by the "committal," a second service, which is held at the graveside as the person is committed to the earth and God's safe keeping. The words taken from the book of Genesis, which remind everyone that they came from dust and will return to

ABOVE: In many churches the coffin is placed in the church on the day before burial to allow friends and relatives to pray for the dead.

dust, are read. Since most Christians allow cremation as well as burial, this second service may also take place at the crematorium.

IN THE GLOSSARY

Anglican Church ✣ Anglo-Catholic
Bible ✣ Heaven ✣ Hell ✣ Icon
John the Baptist ✣ Mary
Orthodox Church ✣ Priest ✣ Protestant
Purgatory ✣ Requiem Mass ✣ Roman
Catholic Church ✣ Sermon

CELEBRATIONS

*"We all gather on the day of the
sun, for it is the first day when
God, separating matter from
darkness, made the world; and on
this same day Jesus Christ our
Savior rose from the dead."*

ST. JUSTIN

5.1
THE CHRISTIAN YEAR

The "Christian Year" [sometimes called the "Liturgical Year"] is a pattern of festivals and celebrations that are observed, to a greater or lesser extent, by the different Christian Churches. In addition to the Christian Year there are many smaller festivals that the Roman Catholic and Orthodox Churches, in particular, celebrate. The majority of these are to do with saints or particular beliefs, such as the Assumption of the Virgin Mary into heaven, which are held by some Churches but not by others. Protestant Churches celebrate the main festivals, such as Christmas and Easter, but not the secondary ones such as Advent and Lent.

THE THREE MAIN CYCLES OF THE CHRISTIAN CHURCH:

a. THE CHRISTMAS CYCLE. The Christian Year begins with the first Sunday of Advent at the end of November. There are four Sundays altogether in Advent, culminating in the feast that celebrates the birth of Jesus in

LEFT: *The entry of Jesus into Jerusalem on a donkey is commemorated by celebrations and processions on Palm Sunday.*

Catechism of the Catholic Church

"Beginning with the Easter Triduum as its source of light, the new age of the Resurrection fills the whole liturgical year with its brilliance. Gradually, on either side of this source, the year is transfigured by the liturgy. It really is 'a year of the Lord's favor.'"

Bethlehem - Christmas - on December 25th. During Advent, Christians look forward to the "coming" of Jesus. Epiphany then follows on January 6th, recalling the time when the Wise Men visited the infant Jesus [Matthew 2.1-12] so becoming the first non-Jews [Gentiles] to play a part in the story of Jesus. It is on this day, however, that many of the Orthodox Churches celebrate the birth of Jesus since that is the traditional date of Christmas.

b. THE EASTER CYCLE. The Easter Cycle is the most important for all Christians because it celebrates the events that led up to the death and resurrection of Jesus. It starts about six weeks after Epiphany with Ash Wednesday, which is the beginning of the season of Lent. On the day before, Shrove Tuesday, Christians have traditionally "shriven" themselves by confessing their sins and seeking absolution from the priest before the fast of Lent begins. During the 40 days of Lent, Christians prepare themselves for Easter by reading their Bibles and praying more than usual in order to focus their hearts and minds around the two events that are at the center of their faith - the death and resurrection of Jesus.

Easter is described in the Church calendar as a "moveable feast." Whereas the date of Christmas is fixed, the dates in the Easter Cycle vary from year to year. For centuries, Easter was the date in the Christian Year when new converts to Christianity were baptized - a custom that was also practiced at Whitsun. Traditionally, at Easter, "alms" were collected for the poor and needy in the Church and prisoners were released from their imprisonment.

ABOVE: Roman Catholics and Orthodox Christians believe that Mary was taken up directly into heaven without experiencing death. This event, the Assumption of the Virgin Mary, is celebrated by both Churches - although on different days.

IN THE GLOSSARY

Advent ✤ All Saints' Day
Ascension Day ✤ Ash Wednesday
Assumption of the Virgin Mary
Bethlehem ✤ Bible ✤ Cathedral
Christmas ✤ Day of Pentecost
Easter ✤ Epiphany ✤ Gentile
Good Friday ✤ Heaven ✤ Lent
Orthodox Church
Protestant Church
Roman Catholic Church ✤ Saint
Shrove Tuesday ✤ Sunday
Whitsun

The time of preparation and privation for Easter starts on Ash Wednesday and runs through to Good Friday. The traditional fast was lifted only on the fourth Sunday of Lent, Mothering Sunday, when people working away from home returned to their nearest cathedral or "mother church" for the day. On Good Friday, the most solemn day in the Christian year, Christians spend lengthy periods of time in church meditating on the death of Jesus. Two days later, though, the mood changes as Christians throughout the world celebrate the return of Jesus from the dead on Easter Day. In the Western Church this day has always fallen on the Sunday following the first full moon on or after March 21st. With Easter Day the Easter Cycle is complete.

c. THE WHITSUN CYCLE. This third cycle, less important than the other two, is based on the day set apart in the Church for remembering the events of the Day of Pentecost - and the birth of the Christian Church. Previously, though, on the 40th day after Easter, many Churches have celebrated Ascension Day and this remains one of the days of Holy Obligation [chief feast days] in the Roman Catholic Church. The Roman Catholic Church also has days dedicated to many saints and the Virgin Mary around this time. A comparatively new festival, Harvest, is celebrated by most Churches at the appropriate time and this festival allows the Churches to show their concern for the poor in an appropriate way. Finally, there are other minor festivals such as Trinity Sunday and All Saints' Day, which some, but by no means all, Christian Churches celebrate.

5.2
SUNDAY

Since most of the early Christians were Jews it was natural for them to continue worshiping in the local synagogue on the Sabbath Day, the Jewish holy day. According to the Bible, God created the world in six days and rested on the seventh, blessing this day and making it holy. In the Ten Commandments, work was forbidden on the Sabbath for this reason, as well as to give slaves and animals a day of rest. Later Jewish tradition classified 39 different kinds of work to be avoided on the Sabbath, and the celebration of this day still forms the basis of Jewish life. A Jewish tradition says that if the whole of Israel celebrated the Sabbath perfectly just once then their Messiah would come.

SUNDAY

For the early Christians Sunday - the day on which Jesus rose from the dead - soon took the place of the Sabbath as the day set aside for worship. To begin with they worshiped on Saturday evenings, as the Sabbath drew to a close, but under the Emperor Trajan, in the third century, these meetings became illegal. By moving the celebration of the Lord's Supper to Sunday morning, the Christian Church severed its last remaining tie with the Jewish religion. Sunday became the Lord's Day, and the Russian Orthodox Church still calls it "Voskresnie" [Resurrection

Genesis 2.3

"He blessed the seventh day and set it apart as a special day, because by that day he had completed his creation and stopped working."

Exodus 20.8

"Observe the Sabbath and keep it holy. You have six days in which to do your work, but the seventh day is a day of rest dedicated to me. On that day no one is to work - neither you, your children, your slaves, your animals, nor the foreigners who live in your country. In six days I, the Lord, made the earth, the sky, the sea, and everything in them, but on the seventh day I rested. That is why I, the Lord, blessed the Sabbath and made it holy."

Day]. Under the Christian Roman Emperor, Constantine, all work was stopped on Sunday and the Law Courts were closed although agricultural work was exempt from restriction. The name "Sunday" was retained even though it was linked directly to the worship of the sun-god in pre-Christian times.

In the Middle Ages attendance at Mass became compulsory in Britain, and after the Reformation Protestants imposed a strict discipline on Sunday throughout Europe. During the 18th century, Evangelical Movements brought about the closure of all places of entertainment and amusement on Sunday. The recent Catechism of the Catholic Church, published in 1994, placed Catholics under a strict obligation to attend Mass each Sunday. This makes Sunday "the foremost holy day of obligation in the universal Church."

The obligation, though, can be discharged by attending Mass on a Saturday evening if that is preferred. In the same year new laws in Britain replaced the old archaic regulations, which had continued by default. Almost all restrictions were lifted from Sunday although large stores were still only allowed to open on the day for a maximum of six hours' trading.

LEFT: Attending a place of worship still remains the main activity for Christians on Sunday although the character of the remainder of the day has changed radically in most countries in recent years.

IN THE GLOSSARY

Bible ✤ Eucharist ✤ Evangelical
Holy Spirit ✤ Lord's Supper
Mass ✤ Protestant ✤ Reformation
Sabbath Day ✤ Sunday ✤ Synagogue
Ten Commandments

St. Justin, second-century Christian leader

"We all gather on the day of the sun, for it is the first day when God, separating matter from darkness, made the world; and on this same day Jesus Christ our Savior rose from the dead."

The Catechism of the Catholic Church

"Participation in the communal celebration of the Sunday Eucharist is a testimony of belonging and of being faithful to Christ and his Church. The faithful give witness by this to their communion in faith and charity. Together they testify to God's holiness and their hope of salvation. They strengthen one another under the guidance of the Holy Spirit."

The Catechism emphasizes the importance of leisure activity and recognizes that Sunday will be the day when this will take place for most people. This is a very suitable use of the day as long as obligations to God and the Church are met first. At the same time those who rest and relax should be mindful of others "who have the same needs and the same rights, yet cannot rest from work because of poverty and misery." They should also remember those who have to work on Sunday to provide the rest and relaxation that others need.

5.3
CHRISTMAS

The Christian Year begins with the first Sunday in Advent, the fourth Sunday before Christmas Day. For 1,400 years, this has been a period of spiritual preparation before the celebration of the birth of Jesus. For many Christians Advent, a time of "comings," is the time to remember.

ADVENT

The period of Advent is a time for Christians to consider the following:

a. THE COMING OF JOHN THE BAPTIST. John is presented in the Gospels as the messenger sent by God to prepare the people for the coming of the Messiah, Jesus. The birth of John, the cousin of Jesus, was seen as a miracle since his parents, Elizabeth and Zechariah, were well beyond normal child-bearing age. Zechariah himself was a prophet and he had some words to say about the role of his son in the ministry of Jesus.

b. THE COMING OF THE MESSIAH, JESUS. This coming was foretold by the prophets in the Old Testament. Readings from the prophets are an important feature of Advent services. Then there

Luke 1. 76-79

*"You, my child, will be called a prophet
of the Most High God,
You will go ahead of the Lord,
to prepare his road for him,
to tell his people that they will be saved
by having their sins forgiven."*

was the "coming" of the Angel Gabriel to the Virgin Mary announcing that she was to give birth to the Messiah [an event called the "Annunciation"].

c. THE SECOND "COMING" OF JESUS. Ever since Jesus left the earth after his resurrection, Christians have been expecting him to return. The disciples of Jesus expected it to happen in their lifetimes. Christians have been waiting for it ever since and are reminded of this during Advent.

CHRISTMAS

At the festival of Christmas [Old English: "Christes Masse"] Christians celebrate a

RIGHT: According to the New Testament, Mary and Joseph traveled to Bethlehem, where Jesus was born. Several years later they returned to live in Nazareth, where Jesus grew up.

The Apostles' Creed

"I believe in Jesus Christ, his only Son, our Lord. He was conceived by the power of the Holy Spirit and born of the Virgin Mary."

central part of their faith - that God became a man in the form of Jesus of Nazareth. This belief is called the "Incarnation." Many Christians believe that Jesus was not conceived by any human father but by God in the form of the Holy Spirit - a miraculous event called "The Virgin Birth" [see 8.4].

Throughout the world Christians come together on Christmas Eve to celebrate Midnight Mass with great thanksgiving. The church is lavishly decorated for this service, which is, in most churches, the best attended of the year. Yet the idea of God being born to a virgin is very difficult to understand. To help them absorb the

RIGHT: The Church has taught that the conception and birth of Jesus were different. The doctrine of the Virgin Birth was intended to convey the belief that Jesus did not share the "original sin" of other human beings.

deeper meaning of the festival, Orthodox Christians use icons of the Virgin and child in their prayers. Statues of the Madonna and child, prominent in Roman Catholic Churches, are visual reminders of the miracle that Christians believe is the heart of the message of Christmas.

EPIPHANY

The word "Epiphany" means "to show forth." In the Eastern Orthodox Church, Epiphany celebrates three manifestations ["showings forth"] of Christ. The first refers to the birth of Jesus when he was shown to the shepherds and Wise Men to be the Savior of the world. The second came later at the baptism of Jesus when he was shown to be God's Son and God blessed him for the work that lay ahead. The third celebrates the first miracle of Jesus when he changed water into wine at Cana, and announced that he had come to usher in God's Kingdom [John 2.1-11].

IN THE GLOSSARY

Advent ✣ Annunciation
Apostles' Creed ✣ Baptism ✣ Christmas
Eastern Orthodox Church ✣ Epiphany
Gentile ✣ Gospels ✣ Holy Spirit
Icon ✣ Incarnation ✣ Isaiah
John the Baptist ✣ Mary ✣ Messiah
Old Testament ✣ Orthodox Church
Prophet ✣ Protestant
Roman Catholic Church ✣ Virgin Birth

In Roman Catholic and Protestant Churches, however, Epiphany is linked with the visit of the Wise Men [Magi] to see Jesus and the "showing" of Jesus to them - the first Gentiles to recognize Jesus as the Savior of the world. Throughout his ministry Jesus made it clear that he was sent first to the Jews and then to the Gentiles.

5.4
LENT

There is no festival in the Christian Year between Epiphany and Ash Wednesday. This is the first day of the season of Lent, a time of fasting and spiritual preparation for Easter, which lasts for 40 days through to Good Friday. In the Orthodox Church, however, the beginning of Lent is preceded by four weeks of fasting ["the Great Fast"]. In the Roman Catholic Church, since 1966, the obligation to fast has been limited to the first day of Lent and Good Friday. Holy Week draws Lent to a close beginning on Palm Sunday and running through until Easter Sunday. Protestants celebrate only the most important days during this time - Palm Sunday, Good Friday, and Easter Day.

LENT

Lent provides a lengthy run-up to the great Christian festival of Easter. According to Matthew [4.1-11] Jesus had just been baptized by John the Baptist in the Jordan River when "the Spirit led him into the desert to be tempted by the Devil" [Matthew 4.1].

During this time, which lasted, according to the Gospels, for 40 days, Jesus fasted, and going without food has traditionally been an important part of

Robert Herrick

"To starve thy sin,
Not bin, And that's to keep thy Lent."

RIGHT: *On Ash Wednesday, the first day of Lent, the priest or minister uses ashes to mark a cross on the forehead of each member of the congregation. The ashes come from burning the palms used in the previous Palm Sunday.*

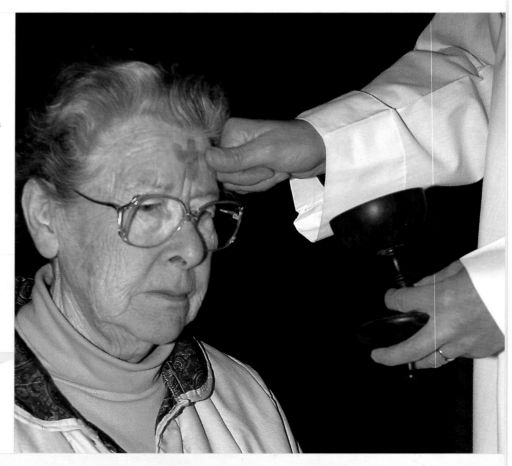

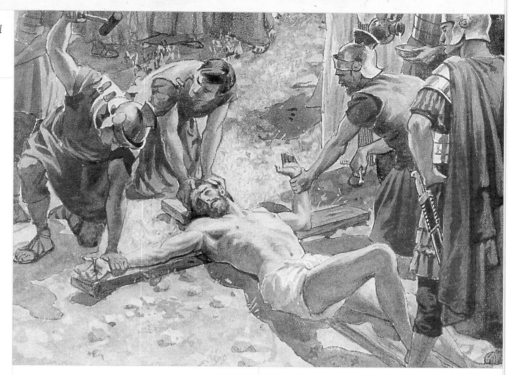

RIGHT: Lent is a season of fasting and self-denial as a way of mourning the death of Jesus, which is remembered on Good Friday.

Lent. In the past, in preparation for Lent, the people would eat up all the fat in the house on the day before Ash Wednesday, Shrove Tuesday. The fat was often used to make pancakes thereby providing a last opportunity for the people to enjoy a feast before the fast began. Shrove Tuesday still remains, although its religious significance has largely disappeared.

On Ash Wednesday a special Eucharist is held in most Catholic, Anglican, and Orthodox Churches. During this service ash, a traditional symbol of penitence, is smeared in the form of a cross on the forehead of each worshiper. The ash for this has been obtained by burning the palm crosses from the previous Palm Sunday. In the Old Testament people used to wear "sackcloth and ashes" as a sign of repentance for their past actions or to show that they were entering a period of mourning. The two themes of repentance and mourning are at the heart of the preparations of Lent. As the priest applies the ash to each worshiper he or she tells them: "Remember O man that dust thou art and to dust shalt thou return," and these same words are also used in the Christian burial service.

Few Protestant Christians now fast, although some Christians, particularly Roman Catholics, try to carry out some form of self-denial during Lent. In most Churches, though, the time is now set aside for serious thought, prayer, and Bible-study. This makes Lent a positive time of spiritual preparation for the death and resurrection of Jesus.

MOTHERING SUNDAY

The fourth Sunday of Lent in the Western Church calendar is "Mothering Sunday." The term "mothering" here refers to three separate things:

✢ The old Bible reading set aside for this day referred to the heavenly city of Jerusalem as the "mother" of all: "But the heavenly Jerusalem is free, and she is our mother" [Galatians 4.26].

✢ The practice in the Middle Ages of the congregations of small churches and chapels visiting either their "mother" or parish church or the "mother church" of their diocese, the cathedral, for spiritual refreshment.

✢ The custom of people visiting their mothers on this day with presents.

For a long time this day was also known as "Refreshment Sunday." This may have been due to the fact that the fast was relaxed on this day to allow the eating of such delicacies as simnel-cakes. The name might, though, owe something to the fact that, until 1969, the Bible reading set aside for this day in the Roman Catholic Church was the miracle of feeding the five thousand men, women, and children. This remains the reading in the Anglican Book of Common Prayer.

IN THE GLOSSARY

Anglican Church ✢ Ash Wednesday
Bible ✢ Book of Common Prayer
Cathedral ✢ Easter ✢ Epiphany
Eucharist ✢ Good Friday ✢ Gospels
Holy Week ✢ Jerusalem
John the Baptist ✢ Lent
Old Testament ✢ Orthodox Church
Palm Sunday ✢ Priest ✢ Protestant
Roman Catholic Church

5.5
HOLY WEEK

The long time of preparation and waiting for the celebrations of Easter is almost over. Events in the Gospels, and in the Church, moved rapidly toward their climax in the city of Jerusalem where Jesus was to meet his death. Holy Week, the week leading up to Easter, begins with Palm Sunday.

PALM SUNDAY

In the time of Jesus, Jews traveled from all over the Roman Empire to Jerusalem for Passover, or Pesach. At Passover every Jew remembered the time, hundreds of years earlier, when their ancestors had escaped from Egyptian slavery through the intervention of God. It was natural for

Zechariah 9.9

"Rejoice, rejoice people of Zion [Jerusalem]!
Shout for joy, you people of Jerusalem!
Look, your king is coming to you!
He comes triumphant and victorious,
but humble and riding on a donkey."

Jesus, as a Jew, to join the pilgrims making their way to Jerusalem. On the outskirts of the city Jesus sent two disciples to find a donkey tethered in a nearby village. The disciples brought the animal back to Jesus. They spread their cloaks over it and Jesus climbed up. The people, realizing something special was going on, spread their cloaks on the road while others cut down palm branches to spread out in front

ABOVE: *This stained-glass window shows Mary Magdalene washing Jesus' feet. To wash someone's feet is a powerful symbol of service to others.*

of Jesus. The crowd shouted out: "Praise to David's Son! God bless him who comes in the name of the Lord! Praise God!" [Matthew 21.9].

On Palm Sunday, many church services end with a procession out of church led by a donkey, often carrying a small child, with the congregation singing and waving small palm crosses. The people are reminded that Jesus was fulfilling prophecies from the Old Testament when he arrived on a donkey in Jerusalem. He rode on a donkey rather than on a horse, which was a military animal, to show that he had come in peace. It was not his intention to overthrow the Romans by force. The Jewish prophet, Isaiah, had spoken of a future kingdom in which a lion would lie down peacefully with a lamb. That was the Kingdom of God that Jesus had come to establish.

MAUNDY THURSDAY

Taken from the Latin word *mandatum*, which means "order," Maundy Thursday reminds us of the "new commandment" that Jesus gave to his disciples. Two events in the Gospels on this day have affected Christian worship:

a. JESUS WASHED THE FEET OF HIS DISCIPLES - the responsibility of the most menial servant in an Eastern household. By washing the feet of his disciples Jesus taught them an important lesson about the Kingdom of God. A disciple must place himself, or herself, at the service of others. Following the example of Jesus the Pope, and other Christian leaders, often wash the feet of others on this day. On Maundy Thursday Catholic priests are reminded of their ordination promise to serve their people by consecrating the bread and wine for their spiritual nourishment. They celebrate the Eucharist on Maundy Thursday with the bishop of the diocese.

John 13.34, 35

"And now I give you a new commandment: love one another. As I have loved you, so you must love one another. If you have love for one another, then everyone will know that you are my disciples."

At this service the bishop consecrates the oil that is going to be used in the sacraments throughout his diocese during the coming year.

b. THE LAST SUPPER OF JESUS with his disciples is remembered. It appears likely that this was a Passover meal that Jesus celebrated with his disciples but this was a Passover with a difference. Jesus instructed his followers to break bread and drink wine in memory of his forthcoming death. This is the origin of the service of Holy Communion [the Eucharist, the Mass, the Divine Liturgy] which stands at the heart of most Christian worship.

During the Eucharist held in most churches on Maundy Thursday the priest wears white vestments and the Gloria is sung for the first time since Ash Wednesday. During the Gloria the bells are rung before falling silent until Holy Saturday - the day between Good Friday and Easter Sunday. In Roman Catholic churches the altar is bare and empty while members of the congregation maintain a vigil in the side-chapel - just as the disciples were asked to do in the Garden of Gethsemane.

ABOVE: *This 15th-century wall painting shows Jesus with his Apostles at the Last Supper, the night before he was crucified.*

IN THE GLOSSARY

Altar ✤ Ash Wednesday ✤ Bishop
Disciple ✤ Divine Liturgy ✤ Easter
Eucharist ✤ Exodus ✤ Good Friday
Gospels ✤ Holy Communion
Jerusalem ✤ Kingdom of God ✤ Mass
Maundy Thursday ✤ Old Testament
Palm Sunday ✤ Passover ✤ Pesach
Priest ✤ Roman Catholic Church

5.6
EASTER

For all Christians, Good Friday is the most solemn day of the year, when they remember the death of Jesus. Often their shared grief draws them together across denominational barriers as they take part in processions, led by someone carrying a cross, reenacting the last few hours in the life of Jesus.

GOOD FRIDAY IN CHURCH

Special services are held in many churches on this day, which used to be called "Black Friday." Often the service runs from noon through to three o'clock in the afternoon as worshipers meditate on the last few hours in the life of Jesus through prayers and readings from one of the Gospels - usually John's. The decor of many churches reflects the somber spirit of the day, with moveable items being removed and permanent ones covered. There are no flowers in church on Good Friday and the Eucharist is not celebrated - that must wait until Easter Sunday.

Each Church has its own distinctive way of celebrating the day. Amongst the most interesting are the following:

a. VISITING THE STATIONS OF THE CROSS in a Roman Catholic Church. There are 14 such Stations [carvings or drawings] in each Catholic church indicating those places where, according to the Bible and tradition, Jesus stopped on his way from Pilate's Judgment-Hall to death on the cross. At each Station, the worshiper stops, kneels, and recites appropriate prayers. At three o'clock, when the death of Jesus is thought to have happened, a covered cross is placed in the center of the church and slowly unveiled as members of the congregation prostrate themselves before it. This is called "venerating the cross."

b. IN ORTHODOX CHURCHES, where Good Friday is known as "Great Friday," the priest carries an icon of the dead Christ and lowers it into a stand in the middle of the church. The people gather around it with candles as if they were at a funeral. Later, the icon is carried around the outside of the church in a funeral procession as the church bell tolls.

In the Orthodox and Catholic Churches, the time between Good Friday and Easter Day - Holy Saturday - is a time of quiet anticipation. Churches are thoroughly cleaned and the best altar-linen and vessels laid out for Easter Day.

EASTER DAY

All Churches hold special services on Easter Day to celebrate the resurrection of Jesus from the dead. Some, though, have a very distinctive way of announcing that the body of Jesus is no longer in the tomb. In Orthodox Churches there is a coffin in church on Holy Saturday to remind worshipers of the dead body of Jesus. Late in the evening, all worshipers leave while the church is plunged into darkness. On the stroke of midnight the Paschal Candle is lit, the priest shouts out "Christ is risen" and the people reply "He is risen indeed." The candle is then carried into the darkened church with the people following close behind. Each person is carrying a candle and as these are gradually lit, the church is filled with light.

Mark's description of the crucifixion [15.22-27]

"They took Jesus to a place called Golgotha, which means 'The Place of the Skull'. There they tried to give him wine mixed with a drug called myrrh but Jesus would not drink it. Then they crucified him and divided his clothes amongst themselves, throwing dice to see who would get which piece of clothing. It was nine o'clock in the morning when they crucified him. The notice of the accusation against him said: 'The King of the Jews.' They also crucified two bandits with Jesus, one on his right and the other on his left."

RIGHT: This church window shows an angel announcing that Jesus has risen from the dead.

1 Corinthians 15.15-17

"…if it is true that the dead are not raised then he did not raise Christ. For if the dead are not raised, neither has Christ been raised. And if Christ has not been raised then your faith is a delusion and you are still lost in your sins."

The throwing open of the church door on the stroke of midnight symbolizes the rolling away of the stone from the door of the tomb. The light dispelling the darkness of the church is a symbol of the power of the resurrection overcoming the darkness in the world. The passing of the light from one person to another symbolizes the passing of the Good News of the Gospel from one to another. The Paschal Candle is lit for every service from Ascension Day to Whitsun. In Roman Catholic Churches a baby is often baptized in the service to symbolize the new life that is at the heart of Easter Day.

Many Christians in Protestant Churches are up early on Easter morning for a "sunrise service." This was the time that the women in the Gospel story went to the tomb to anoint the body of Jesus after the end of the Sabbath Day only to find it empty. The sun rising over the horizon is a suitable symbol of the new life that the resurrection of Christ brings to everyone. In this way the tone is set for the rest of the Christian Year since the resurrection of Jesus by the power of God is the foundation of the Christian Gospel.

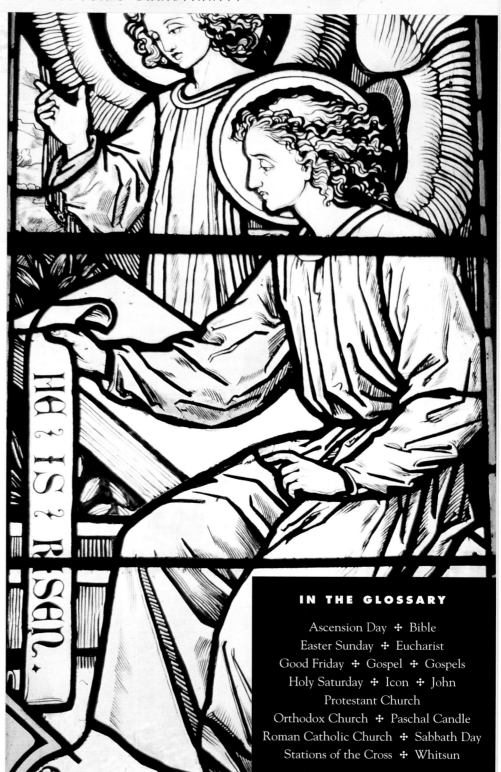

IN THE GLOSSARY

Ascension Day ✤ Bible
Easter Sunday ✤ Eucharist
Good Friday ✤ Gospel ✤ Gospels
Holy Saturday ✤ Icon ✤ John
Protestant Church
Orthodox Church ✤ Paschal Candle
Roman Catholic Church ✤ Sabbath Day
Stations of the Cross ✤ Whitsun

5.7
AFTER EASTER

Easter brings to a close the two main cycles of the Christian Year. There are still some important festivals to come, though, and these center around Pentecost which celebrates the giving of the Holy Spirit to the first disciples in Jerusalem [Acts 2.1-8]. Before Pentecost comes Ascension Day.

ASCENSION DAY

The Gospels tell us that Jesus, after returning from the dead, spent 40 days making various "appearances" to his disciples and other groups of followers. He then left the earth and his disciples altogether and "he was taken up to heaven as they watched him, and a cloud hid him from their sight" [Acts 1.9].

It is this event that some Christians, but by no means all, celebrate 40 days after Easter on Ascension Day. Protestant Churches, such as Baptist and Methodist Churches, do not celebrate the day, but in the Roman Catholic Church it is a Holy Day [a Day of Obligation]. At the special Mass on Ascension Day, Catholics are encouraged to wait another ten days, when they will be able to celebrate the giving of the Holy Spirit at Pentecost.

PENTECOST

Fifty days after Easter the Church celebrates Pentecost and the giving of the Holy Spirit. This day, often called "the birthday of the Christian Church," initiated a period of intense evangelistic activity in which, on the first day alone, 3,000 people were added to the Church.

RIGHT: A 14th-century painting showing Christ's ascension into heaven after Pentecost, with the disciples and Mary looking on.

Luke 24. 50-53

"Then he led them out of the city as far as Bethany, where he raised his hands and blessed them. As he was blessing them, he departed from them and was taken up into heaven. They worshiped him and went back into Jerusalem, filled with great joy, and spent all their time in the Temple giving thanks to God."

Acts 2. 1-4

"When the Day of Pentecost came, all the believers were gathered together in one place. Suddenly there was a noise from the sky which sounded like a strong wind blowing, and it filled the whole house where they were sitting. Then they saw what looked like tongues of fire which spread out and touched each person there. They were all filled with the Holy Spirit and began to talk in other languages, as the Spirit enabled them to speak."

LEFT: Although a harvest festival was celebrated by Jews, it is only comparatively recently that it has been celebrated by the Christian Church.

Traditionally the festival carries two names:

✠ Pentecost. This is the name of the old Jewish harvest festival ["the Feast of Weeks"] with the word itself means "fifty." This festival always fell 50 days after the great festival of Pesach at which the deliverance of the Jews from slavery in Egypt, an event known as the Exodus, was commemorated.

✠ Whitsun. This name is taken from "White Sunday" since this was the traditional time in the Church when new converts to the Christian faith were baptized. For this ceremony they wore white clothes as a symbol of their new purity through faith in Christ. In some Churches this custom is maintained as people are confirmed on this day. During this service the bishop lays his hands on the head of the person and prays that the Holy Spirit might come into his or her life.

HARVEST

Since the middle of the 19th century many Christian Churches have celebrated Harvest festival at the appropriate time of the year. For this festival the church is decorated with harvest produce, which is distributed to the poor after the service. The Harvest service provides an opportunity for worshipers to thank God for all the things he has provided for them, and others, in the natural world.

OTHER FESTIVALS

There are two important festivals, celebrated by the Roman Catholic Church, which follow each other on November 1st and 2nd. On All Saints' Day, November 1st, all of those saints who are now enjoying their rest with God in paradise are remembered. On this day Catholics are encouraged to pray to the saints for assistance in their everyday lives

and to follow the examples that such men and women of God have set. On the following day, All Souls' Day, the souls of those who are in purgatory are remembered. In some churches three Masses are said on this day but for most Catholics All Souls' Day is an opportunity to remember that heaven lies beyond purgatory and this is the final destination of all who believe.

IN THE GLOSSARY

All Saints' Day ✠ All Souls' Day
Ascension Day ✠ Baptist Church
Bishop ✠ Disciples ✠ Easter ✠ Exodus
Gospels ✠ Holy Spirit ✠ Jerusalem
Mass ✠ Methodist Church
Protestant Church ✠ Pentecost
Pesach ✠ Purgatory
Roman Catholic Church ✠ Saint
Whitsun

PRAYER AND WORSHIP

"We all have the need to worship...True Christian worship can never let us be indifferent to the needs of others, to the cries of the hungry, of the naked and homeless, of the sick and the prisoners, of the oppressed and disadvantaged."

ARCHBISHOP DESMOND TUTU

6.1
CHRISTIAN WORSHIP

In every act of Christian worship God must remain unknowable, a mystery, and this evokes a feeling of awe in the worshiper. God's transcendence places him beyond human reach and all language about God remains totally inadequate. Much of the words and music of worship emphasize this other-worldliness of God. Yet, paradoxically, people find themselves drawn toward God through worship. Worship makes God accessible. The hymns, the Bible readings, the prayers, and the sermon are all intended to awaken these feelings. The religious philosopher Rudolf Otto underlined this at the turn of the century when he said that the Christian God was "Mysterious, overwhelming, and fascinating."

PATTERNS OF WORSHIP

For centuries there have been two broad styles of Christian worship and these are still found in the Church today:

a. THE LITURGICAL APPROACH. The worship of some Churches, such as the Roman Catholic, Orthodox, and Anglican Churches, follows strict patterns of worship [called the "liturgy"]. The liturgies are laid out clearly in different Prayer Books for congregations to follow. In the Anglican Church, for example, the Book of Common Prayer or the Alternative Service Book is used, while Roman Catholic congregations follow the Missal during their services. In those services that follow the liturgical approach the emphasis is very much on form, ritual, and pattern. Hymns and some of the prayers introduce the only note of variety from week to week. People feel comfortable and at ease with a liturgy that is very familiar to them.

Liturgies also include a number of symbolic elements, many of which can be

---

Early Christian worship
- Acts 2.42, 43

"They spent their time in learning from the apostles, taking part in the fellowship, and sharing in the fellowship meals and the prayers. Many miracles and wonders were done through the apostles, and everyone was filled with awe."

RIGHT: Quaker services are unlike any other kind. Silence is valued above everything else as a means of worship.

Archbishop Desmond Tutu

"We all have the need to worship…True Christian worship can never let us be indifferent to the needs of others, to the cries of the hungry, of the naked and homeless, of the sick and the prisoners, of the oppressed and disadvantaged."

clearly seen in the central Christian service of the Eucharist. The approach of liturgical Churches is likely to be sacramental, with a high level of dependence in worship on the sacraments.
b. THE PROTESTANT APPROACH The approach of Protestant Churches to worship is very different. These Churches do not have a Prayer Book since they claim that following a strict liturgy prevents the Holy Spirit from operating with freedom in their worship. In Protestant services the emphasis is on hymn and chorus singing, and many new hymns have been written in recent years; extempore prayers that follow no set pattern; readings from the Bible; and the preaching of the Word - the sermon. Although most Protestant Churches practice Holy Communion and Baptism, the emphasis is on the spoken and written word. Preaching and teaching of the Bible are central to Protestant worship. Often art, poetry, dance, and other creative means are used within services to put over the Christian message.

OTHER APPROACHES

There are, of course, groups of Christians who do not fit into either of the above broad patterns of worship. The Society of

Friends [Quakers] place a very high degree of importance on silence in their worship. Most of Sunday worship is silent as people meditate and think about spiritual matters. The silence is broken only when someone feels prompted by the Holy Spirit to speak.

The Charismatic Movement grew out of the main denominations in the 1960s. It is based on the belief that the Holy Spirit can give a person the gift to prophesy to the church; speak or pray in an unknown language [speaking in tongues]; interpret the unknown language; and heal members of the congregation who are sick. Although Charismatic Christians are found in all of the main Churches, they are associated mostly with the Pentecostal Movement, which has a substantial following in the United States and Britain.

Many of those associated with the Charismatic Movement belong to the House-Church Movement. This is made up of people who, since the 1970s, have become dissatisfied with existing Churches and have formed their own small

ABOVE: Church worship is a very imprecise and inadequate attempt to express the inexpressible about God.

fellowship groups without any denominational allegiance. Because they study the Bible, sing hymns, pray, and break bread together they see themselves going back to the pattern of worship found in the New Testament.

IN THE GLOSSARY

Alternative Service Book
Anglican Church ✤ Baptism ✤ Bible
Book of Common Prayer
Charismatic Movement ✤ Eucharist
Holy Communion ✤ Holy Spirit
House-Church Movement ✤ Liturgy
Missal ✤ New Testament
Orthodox Church
Protestant Church ✤ Quakers
Roman Catholic Church ✤ Sacrament
Sermon ✤ Society of Friends
Speaking in Tongues

6.2

ROMAN CATHOLIC CHURCHES

Although Roman Catholic churches were traditionally built in the shape of a cross, many of the new ones are semicircular or circular in design. This change is intended to signify a theological message. The new churches stress the equality of all people in God's presence, with the people of God gathered around the altar. The altar is the place where God meets with his people, so the most appropriate place for it is in the middle of the congregation. The Second Vatican Council [1963-65] decreed that the high altar should be moved away from the wall in traditional churches so that the priest can stand behind it and face the people as he celebrates Mass.

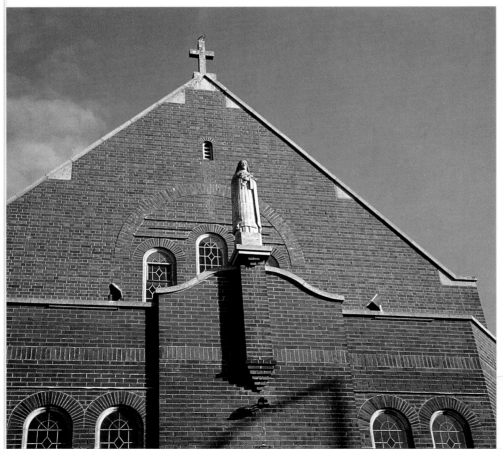

HOLY WATER

Just inside the door of a Catholic church worshipers find a small container of holy water into which they dip two fingers to trace the "sign of the cross" on their bodies. The fingers move from head to breast and across the shoulders from left to right [in the Eastern Churches the hand moves from right to left]. The worshiper mutters the words "In the name of the Father and of the Son, and of the Holy Spirit." The water, which has been blessed by a priest, symbolizes the new life that all can expect to find in the Church.

BAPTISMAL FONT

This new life is also symbolized by the font, which is also placed just inside the church door. This is the stone receptacle

LEFT: *Modern churches are no longer built in the shape of a cross; however, the cross is still a major feature in most church buildings.*

that holds the water when a baby is baptized. The oldest fonts were in the shape of a "grave" with three steps down, where the person to be baptized "died with Christ and rose with him to a new life" after immersion in the water. The position of the font is a reminder that every person must be baptized before he or she can belong to the fellowship of the Church and share in the salvation that it offers. In some modern churches, though, the font is placed in the middle of the church to underline the idea that Baptism brings a baby into the warmth of the Church family, which then undertakes to cherish, love, and care for it.

THE ALTAR

In traditional churches the altar stands, together with a crucifix and candles, at the end of the nave, or central passageway, in the middle of the east wall. This location was originally chosen so that when worshipers face the altar they are looking in the direction of the rising sun and the holy city of Jerusalem.

A tabernacle [cupboard] stands behind the altar or in a side-chapel holding the Reserved Sacrament, which is used every time the Mass is celebrated - in church or in a person's home. Originally a rood-screen, made of wood or stone, blocked off most of the altar from the gaze of the people but most of these have been long since been removed. The crucifix on the altar contains the figure of Jesus on the cross to help worshipers meditate on his death. Occasionally during the Christian Year, as at Easter, the crucifix is covered with a cloth.

ABOVE: *In Roman Catholic churches, people often light votive candles when they pray. Candles symbolize the light of God, which shines in the hearts of all true believers.*

BELOW: *Catholic churches, and worship, make extensive use of symbols as a way of presenting spiritual truth in a way that people can understand. The crucifix serves as a reminder that Jesus sacrificed his life for us.*

AROUND THE CHURCH

There are carved statues or paintings around the walls of the church showing the 14 Stations of the Cross. The Stations illustrate the different places at which Jesus, according to the Gospels and tradition, stopped on his way to Calvary, the place where he was crucified. Worshipers process around each of the Stations during Holy Week, pausing at each to say a special prayer and remember the sufferings of Jesus.

Statues of the Virgin Mary and other saints occupy an important place in a Roman Catholic church. Mary was the mother of Jesus who, Catholics believe, entered the world sinless and left it without experiencing death [see section 8.4]. Worshipers often light candles in front of her statue as they pray, especially when they are seeking help or guidance. Elsewhere in the church anyone who simply wants to say a prayer is encouraged to light a votive candle. Candles are used widely in Catholic worship to symbolize the light of God, which shines eternally in the world and in the hearts of all true believers.

IN THE GLOSSARY

Altar ✢ Calvary ✢ Crucifix ✢ Easter
Eucharist ✢ Font ✢ Gospels
Holy Week ✢ Jerusalem ✢ Mary
Mass ✢ Nave ✢ Priest
Reserved Sacrament
Roman Catholic Church
Rood-Screen ✢ Saint
Second Vatican Council
Stations of the Cross ✢ Tabernacle
Virgin Mary ✢ Votive Candle

6.3
ORTHODOX CHURCHES

Of the three great Christian "families," the one with which people in Britain and the United States are least familiar is the Orthodox Church. The reason is simple. Few worshipers from this tradition live in these two countries. The majority of the self-governing Churches that belong to the Orthodox family are in Eastern Europe, Russia, and around the eastern side of the Mediterranean. Wherever Orthodox worshipers are found, however, there are sure to be distinctive and beautiful places of worship.

ORTHODOX CHURCHES AND SYMBOLISM

Of all Christian churches, Orthodox buildings rely most heavily on symbolism. The basic plan of most Orthodox churches is a square with a dome above the center. The square symbolizes the Orthodox belief that everything in God's world is orderly and correct. At the same time it encourages everyone to appreciate that they are equal in God's presence. The four corners of the square represent the four Gospels, while the dome symbolizes the heavens stretched out over the earth, represented by the floor of the church.

An important feature of the largest Orthodox buildings is the painting across the ceiling of Christ the Pantocrator [ruler of the heavens, the universe, and the earth]. The High Altar is located in the east wall of the church and is separated from the people in the congregation by the iconostasis. This is a large screen covered with icons [sacred paintings] of Mary, Jesus, and the Apostles. The screen symbolizes the division that can never be crossed between heaven and earth, between God and the human race.

The choir, out of sight in the transepts [the arms of the cross], plays a very important part in Orthodox worship since musical instruments cannot be used. The choir leads the worship of the people.

ICONS

Orthodox Christians believe that God is all-powerful and beyond the reach of human beings. Normally this would make any form of worship impossible. Icons, though, are special religious paintings that bring God within the reach of anyone who

LEFT: The overall atmosphere in an Orthodox church is that of the omnipotence of God.

RIGHT: Icons are one of the most important Christian symbols and are widely used in worship. Recently the use of icons has extended beyond the Orthodox Church.

wishes to worship him. Icons are used as devotional aids both in church and in the home. Each icon is believed to be an earthly copy of a heavenly image, so painting them demands a high level of skill and religious devotion from the artist, for which special training is given.

Icons usually depict saints, the Apostles, or members of the Holy Family - especially Mary and the infant Jesus. Icons usually depict liturgical celebrations rather than actual historical events, though some monasteries do have legends linked with their foundation painted on icons.

There are icons around the walls and ceilings of the church building, and candles are often burned in front of them. Worshipers usually light one of the candles and kiss the icon or prostrate themselves before taking their place in the church congregation. Some icons are thought to have had a miraculous origin - to have been made "without hands" or to have been transported from afar. The symbolism of the icon is believed to affect the presence of the saint or mystery depicted, and it is in that presence that prayer and devotion are made.

IN THE GLOSSARY

Altar ✣ Apostle ✣ Divine Liturgy
Gospels ✣ Icon ✣ Iconostasis
Incarnation ✣ Mary
Monastery ✣ Orthodox Church
Royal Doors ✣ Saint

THE ROYAL DOORS

The iconostasis is the screen that separates the congregation from the altar. Only ordained clergy may pass through the central door [the Royal Doors] of the iconostasis to the altar, although the people are able to glimpse the altar through the Royal Doors. An icon on the left of the iconostasis shows the Incarnation while the one on the right shows the promised return of Jesus. During the Divine Liturgy the communion bread and wine are brought to the people through the Royal Doors. They are told that Christ is in the church through the communion elements, so bringing together the icons on either side of the Royal Doors.

6.4
ANGLICAN CHURCHES

Traditional cross-shaped Anglican churches stand at the heart of most villages and towns in England. In the past these buildings were expected to fulfill two important social functions. They provided consecrated ground surrounding the church in which members of the parish could be buried. They also provided the bells that called members of the parish to worship on Sundays and announced to the community important local, national, and international events.

INSIDE THE BUILDINGS

The older Anglican churches in Britain were taken over from the Roman Catholics at the time of King Henry VIII and it is not surprising to find a close similarity between the buildings of these two denominations. As in Catholic churches so the font in an Anglican church is likely to be found nestled just inside the door since many Anglicans still believe that baptism is the door through which a person must pass to enter the Church. Modern churches, however, use a portable font that can be placed in the middle of the people to show that the child is being welcomed into the Church, and God's, family.

The nave is a passageway that runs almost the entire length of the church; with the pews on each side, where members of the congregation sit. The nave ends at the chancel, which runs at right-angles in front of the altar. This gives most churches their characteristic cross-shape and usually houses one or two side-chapels. Often these side-chapels are

ABOVE: *During an Anglican service, someone stands at the lectern in order to read a passage from the Bible.*

RIGHT: *The traditional parish church is still at the heart of many rural communities providing many important services to the community.*

dedicated to a saint, sometimes the Virgin Mary, and are used for services when the congregation is small.

There are two important pieces of furniture on each side of the chancel:
a. THE PULPIT. This is a platform that is usually reached by steps. The priest goes into the pulpit to deliver his sermon during which a passage from the Bible is explained and discussed. The Anglican Church is a Reformed Church and this means that a strong emphasis is placed on the preaching of the Word [the Bible] - although this emphasis is far more important in Protestant Churches.
b. THE LECTERN. Normally made of wood or stone, the lectern is a reading desk from which the Bible is read during all services. This is often ornately carved with an eagle, reminding members of the congregation of Isaiah's words that those who hope in the Lord "will soar on wings like eagles" [40.31]. Most of the readings from the Bible take place from the lectern but in High Church [Anglo-Catholic] churches the Bible is passed down into the

middle of the congregation before the reading from the Gospels is given. This follows the example of the Roman Catholic Church where this also happens.

The altar is situated in the east wall and a quick glance at this reveals whether the church is Evangelical or Anglo-Catholic - or neither. High Church altars resemble those found in Catholic churches containing several candles and a crucifix. Evangelical altars, on the other hand, are very simple containing little more than a cross, an open Bible, and some flowers. These obvious differences, though, mask much deeper differences of doctrine and worship between these two groups leading many to believe that the Anglican Church is really two Churches rather than one.

Usually altars are made of stone and are situated at the far, east end of the church, although modern churches sometimes place a simple wooden altar or Communion table in the center of the building. This marks a change of emphasis for many Anglicans who now see the Eucharist as a fellowship meal in which everyone shares, rather than a sacrifice offered to God by the priest on behalf of the people. For them the altar represents the table on which Jesus shared his last meal with his disciples.

IN THE GLOSSARY

Altar ✛ Anglican Church
Anglo-Catholic ✛ Baptism ✛ Bible
Eucharist ✛ Gospels ✛ Font
High Church ✛ Lectern ✛ Nave
Protestant Church ✛ Priest
Pulpit ✛ Roman Catholic Church
Saint ✛ Sermon ✛ Virgin Mary

6.5
PROTESTANT CHURCHES

Although the Baptist Church and the Quakers were born in the 17th century, the great Protestant revival took place in the 18th and 19th centuries. This was largely due to the very effective preaching work of John Wesley in Britain and George Whitefield in the United States. Charles Wesley, John's brother, made an equally important contribution to the fledgling Protestant Church by writing more than 1,000 hymns, many of which are still used in worship today. Most of the Protestant places of worship [variously called churches, chapels, meeting-houses, or citadels] were built during this time. In recent years, the newer denominations such as the Pentecostal Church and the House-Churches have erected buildings that reflect their own styles of worship, leaving worshipers free to move around during the services if they wish.

PROTESTANT
PLACES OF WORSHIP

The emphasis in Roman Catholic and Anglican services is on the celebration of the sacraments and this is reflected in their buildings where the focus is the altar. The emphasis in Baptist, Methodist and Presbyterian worship, however, is very strongly on the preaching of the Word of God [the Bible]. There is no altar in a Protestant church, but the pulpit, the place from which the Bible is preached, is the focus of the church. The sermon is the most important part of the service; therefore the pulpit is the most important feature of the Protestant church.

ARIGHT: *Protestants place a great emphasis on the Bible in their worship including the preaching of the "Word of God."*

ARIGHT: Most of the Protestant buildings erected during the 18th and 19th centuries were influenced by the Methodist movement.

Two other features are particularly noticeable in Baptist and Methodist churches:

a. THERE IS A COMMUNION TABLE AT THE FRONT OF THE CHURCH. This holds the individual glasses and pieces of bread that are taken to the people in their seats during the Lord's Supper [Breaking of Bread]. During this service the minister and the elders [deacons] of the church sit behind the table facing the people.

b. IN BAPTIST CHURCHES THERE IS A BAPTISMAL POOL AT THE FRONT, which is opened up and filled with water for the service of Believer's [Adult] Baptism. At other times the pool is empty and covered.

Singing plays a very important part in Protestant services. In some churches singing is led by an organist, although a piano and a music-group are more likely to be used in many churches. Much of the new church music written in recent years emphasizes participation of the congregation in the worship.

MEETING HOUSES AND CITADELS

Quakers [members of the "Society of Friends"] gather together in places of worship that are called "meeting houses." Their worship is largely one of silent reflection and this simplicity is reflected in the rooms in which they meet. The rooms are simple and bare with the chairs arranged in a circle or square around a table, which contains little more than a Bible and some flowers.

Members of the Salvation Army meet for worship in what is known as a citadel. The word means "a small, fortified city" and since the 19th century Salvation Army citadels have been seen as places of refuge and safety from the evil world outside.

Citadels resemble other Protestant places of worship; however, a citadel does not have a Communion table since the Salvation Army does not celebrate Holy Communion. The hall is divided into two main sections:

a. THE UPPER AREA, the rostrum, where the band sits. At the front of this is situated a reading desk from which the officer conducts the service.

b. THE LOWER PART where the congregation sits. The "mercy-seat" or "penitent's form" is a long bench in front of the congregation. Anyone from the congregation can come forward to this bench and kneel if he or she wants to seek God's forgiveness or ask for his help. Uniquely, among Nonconformist Churches, the Salvation Army has a flag and this is displayed prominently in the citadel for all to see.

IN THE GLOSSARY

Altar ✤ Anglican Church
Baptism ✤ Believer's Baptism
Baptist Church ✤ Bible
Breaking of Bread ✤ Citadel ✤ Deacon
Holy Communion ✤ Lectern
Lord's Supper ✤ Methodist Church
Minister ✤ Presbyterian Church
Protestant Church
Presbyterian Church ✤ Pulpit
Quakers ✤ Roman Catholic Church
Sacrament ✤ Salvation Army
Sermon ✤ Society of Friends

6.6
PRAYER AND MEDITATION

Although public prayer is a feature of Christian worship most Christians prefer to pray in private. This is because Jesus encouraged them to do so and prayer is an intensely private matter between God and the worshiper. In the Sermon on the Mount, Jesus told his followers not to pray to gain the admiration of others but to "go to your room, close the door and pray to your Father, who is unseen. And your Father, who sees what you do in private, will reward you" [Matthew 6.6].

Matthew 6.6-13. The Lord's Prayer

"This, then, is how you should pray:
'Our Father in heaven:
May your holy name be honored;
may your Kingdom come;
may your will be done on earth
as it is in heaven.
Give us today the food we need.
Forgive us the wrongs we have done,
as we forgive the wrongs that
others have done to us.
Do not bring us to hard testing,
but keep us safe from the Evil One.'"

PRAYER

The only set prayer that is common to Christians from all traditions and denominations is the Lord's Prayer or the "Our Father" as Catholics call it. This prayer contains those elements that are present, in some shape or form, in almost all Christian prayers:

✢ the praise and adoration of God. Christian prayer invariably begins with the worshiper thanking God for the world He has made and the faculties to enjoy it.

✢ a confession of any sins committed and the forgiveness of God.

✢ requests to God to intervene in their own life and in the lives of others. Prayers that are said for other people are called "intercessions" and these form a central part of both public and private prayer.

✢ thanksgiving for all the blessings that have already been received from God.

When introducing the Lord's Prayer to his disciples Jesus told them: "When you pray, do not use a lot of meaningless words, as the pagans do, who think that their gods will hear them because their prayers are long. Your Father already knows what you need before you ask him. This, then, is how you should pray..." [Matthew 6.6-13].

Unlike many other religions there are no set times for prayer in Christianity - unless you are a monk or a nun. Many Christians, though, do feel the need to start each day with a "Quiet Time" when they set aside moments to read their Bible and pray. They may also end the day in the same way as well.

The Hail Mary

"Hail Mary, full of grace,
the Lord is with thee.
Blessed art thou among women
And blessed is the fruit
of thy womb, Jesus.
Holy Mary, Mother of God,
Pray for us sinners, now
And at the hour of our death. Amen."

MEDITATION AND CONTEMPLATION

The Catholic Church has a very strong monastic tradition that goes back to the fourth century. Both meditation and contemplation belong firmly to this tradition although, in recent years, monks and nuns have made great efforts to share their experiences of prayer with others. Meditation is a form of mental prayer that

involves deep concentration on the presence and activity of God. Meditation, which is practiced in religions other than Christianity, controls the mind and the breathing so that a person can focus on God. Within the Roman Catholic tradition the saints, especially the Virgin Mary, can act as the focus of the thoughts. Some Christians use "visualization" to try to visualize a passage from the Bible to discover its true meaning for themselves.

Contemplation goes a stage further than meditation. Through it a person becomes increasingly aware of the joy and beauty of God. In its most intense form contemplation leads to an ecstatic union between God and the worshiper when he or she loses all physical contact with the world. This experience, called "absorption" or "rapture," has been experienced by such great saints of the past as Teresa of Avila and Julian of Norwich.

ABOVE: In almost every religion the spiritual life is built around prayer, and the Christian faith is no exception.

IN THE GLOSSARY

Bible ✦ Contemplation ✦ Gospels
Intercession ✦ Lord's Prayer
Meditation ✦ Monk ✦ Our Father
Roman Catholic Church ✦ Saint
Sermon on the Mount ✦ Virgin Mary

6.7
AIDS TO PRAYER

The majority of Christians do not make use of any aids to prayer. In the Protestant Churches, for instance, such aids have always been viewed with great suspicion since the clear message of the Reformation was that people could gain clear access to the presence of God themselves. Other Christians, though, especially Roman Catholics and Orthodox believers, find that such aids are very helpful to them in their devotional lives.

Two of the most valuable aids to prayer are the following:

1. THE CRUCIFIX. The cross, the chief symbol of Christianity, was seldom used by Christians before the time of the first Christian Roman Emperor, Constantine, in the fourth century. Under his rule the crucifixion of criminals ceased and Jesus was set forward as the crucified and glorified savior. The symbol of the cross went wherever Christians did, albeit with great variety in its shape and detail. The Latin cross has an upright bar with a single crossbar, while the cross of the Celts in Scotland and Ireland had a circle imposed on it.

Today the cross, in some form, is likely to be found in almost every church of whatever denomination. The crucifix, though, is a cross that carries the crucified figure of Jesus on it. Whether worn around a person's neck or placed on the altar of a church, the crucifix signifies the sufferings of Christ through which Christians believe they are saved.

Galatians 6.14

"As for me, however, I will boast only about the cross of our Lord Jesus Christ; for by means of his cross the world is dead to me and I am dead to the world."

ABOVE: *The cross, the most important symbol in the Christian faith, reminds people of the suffering and death of Jesus.*

Toward the end of Holy Week during Easter the crucifixes in many churches are empty and this signifies the fundamental belief that Jesus has risen from the dead. Among Protestant Churches only the Lutherans occasionally make use of the crucifix. Evangelicals have often considered the crucifix to be idolatrous, suggesting a dead rather than a risen Christ. Therefore, Evangelicals have argued that at best the cross should be empty.

Many Christians have crucifixes and crosses in their homes as well as in churches. This helps them to meditate and think about the death of Jesus. Often they conduct their own personal devotional sessions in front of the crucifix. Many Christians find it very moving to pray in front of a crucifix.

2. THE ROSARY. The rosary is a traditional aid to help people pray and is found most frequently in Roman Catholic churches and homes. It is made up of five sets of ten beads known as decades. Each decade is separated from the next by a single bead. The beads of the rosary are easily distinguishable to the

LEFT: *The rosary is used mainly by Roman Catholics. A certain prayer is said for each bead of the rosary.*

The Gloria Patri

"Glory be to the Father, and to the Son, and to the Holy Spirit. As it was in the beginning, is now and ever shall be, world without end. Amen."

b. THE "SORROWFUL" MYSTERIES. These are events linked with the suffering and death of Jesus including the agony in the Garden of Gethsemane, the crowning with thorns, the carrying of the cross, and the crucifixion.
c. THE "GLORIOUS" MYSTERIES. These include the resurrection and ascension of Jesus and the taking up of Mary bodily into heaven.

Like all forms of meditation, using the rosary is intended to lead the worshiper into a deeper understanding and experience of God. Every Christian is very conscious of the distance that separates him or her from God. Using a crucifix in personal devotions, making one's way through the beads of a rosary, or centering the mind and the soul by using an icon are simply different ways in which Christians attempt to bridge that gap.

touch. A Hail Mary [see section 6.5] is said on each bead of the decade. The Gloria Patri [see right] is said on the single bead. Attached to one of the single beads is a group of three more beads, another single bead, and a cross or a crucifix.

For some Catholics using the rosary ["rose garden"] is as automatic as saying the familiar prayers, of which there are three - the Lord's Prayer or the Pater Noster [see section 6.5], said on the single bead; the Hail Mary, said on each of the

group of three beads; and the Gloria Patri, which is repeated on the single bead that comes to the circle.

While saying their prayers using the rosary each worshiper also contemplates 15 holy "mysteries," or events, associated with the life of Jesus. These mysteries are divided into three groups:
a. THE "JOYFUL" MYSTERIES. These are events associated with the birth and boyhood of Jesus including the Annunciation, Mary's visit to Elizabeth, and the birth of Jesus.

IN THE GLOSSARY
Altar ✣ Annunciation ✣ Crucifix
Easter ✣ Evangelical ✣ Gloria Patri
Hail Mary ✣ Holy Week ✣ Icon
Lord's Prayer ✣ Mary ✣ Orthodox
Church ✣ Pater Noster ✣ Protestant
Reformation ✣ Roman Catholic Church
Saint ✣ Trinity

6.8
CHRISTIAN LEADERS

In most branches of the Christian Church leaders play a very important role but not all Churches have professional, fulltime leaders. There are those Churches, such as the Quakers and Plymouth Brethren, that draw their leaders from among the local congregation. This provides the opportunity for those who are not ordained [laity] to use their gifts for the benefit of the Church. However, only a small minority of Churches work in this way.

Each Church has its own way of training its priests or ministers. The training period is often a long one. The Roman Catholic Church, for instance, takes six years to train its priests. During this time the Church speaks of "testing the vocation" of its ordinands to see whether they are "called" to the work ahead. At the end of his training the

LEFT: *Since the first days of Christianity, Church leaders have played a vital role in guiding people in the correct ways to follow the teachings of Jesus Christ.*

RIGHT: *In the Christian Church, the priest or minister plays a sacramental, preaching, and leadership role.*

Ignatius, second century

"Let everyone revere the deacons as Jesus Christ, the bishop as the image of the Father, and the presbyters [priests] as the senate of God and the assembly of the apostles. For without them one cannot speak of the Church."

Catechism of the Catholic Church, 1567

"Because it is joined with the episcopal order [that of bishops] the office of priest shares in the authority by which Christ himself builds up and sanctifies and rules His Body [the Church]."

priest takes a vow of celibacy, although the Roman Catholic Church is the only major denomination that requires this of its priests.

In the Roman Catholic and Anglican ordination ceremonies bishops lay their hands on the head of each person being ordained. This is to transmit God's Holy Spirit to them for the task that lies ahead. Because each person is believed to need a vocation to enter the priesthood, this is also a recognition that the new priest has received a call from God. Although Free Churches do not have a formal ordination ceremony, they do recognize that a person has been "set aside" by God for the special task that lies ahead.

In the Roman Catholic, Anglican, and Orthodox priesthoods being ordained gives a person authority to dispense the sacraments - especially the Eucharist. A priest alone can dispense the bread and wine which, for Roman Catholics, become the body and blood of Christ in the Mass. In five of the seven sacraments a priest

The Book of Common Prayer

These words are spoken by a bishop to a priest who is being ordained:

"A priest is called by God to work with the bishop and his fellow-priests, as servant and shepherd among the people to whom he is sent. He is to proclaim the word of the Lord, to call his hearers to repentance, and in Christ's name to absolve and to declare the forgiveness of sins. He is to baptise…He is to preside at the celebration of Holy Comunion… He is to lead his people in prayer and worship… He is to minister to the sick and prepare the dying for death."

alone can officiate, but in Infant Baptism any lay person can carry out the sacrament in an emergency, and in marriage the husband and wife dispense the sacrament to each other in the Nuptial Mass.

Within the Roman Catholic tradition, then, the priest carries an authority that is not carried by the priest or minister in any other Church. Indeed in the Protestant Churches, such as Baptist and Methodist, the minister carries largely a preaching and leading role. Beneath him or her is an elected body of elders or deacons who discuss and decide on most matters in the Church.

WOMEN PRIESTS

There are no women priests in the Roman Catholic and Orthodox Churches nor does their ordination seem likely in the foreseeable future. An episcopal letter written by Pope John Paul 11 in May 1994 ruled out the possibility of this ever

happening. At about the same time, the first women were being ordained into the Church of England. Most of the Protestant Churches have had ordained women for a long time, although the number of men in the ministry is far greater than the number of women.

Those opposed to the ordination of women have argued their case largely on the basis of Church tradition and the teaching of the Bible. Those who support the ordination of women have drawn attention to the widely varied work performed by a priest, arguing that women can bring new, and very valuable, insights to much of it. This work includes dispensing the sacraments; conducting services; visiting the sick; preparing people

for Baptism, confirmation, and marriage; helping the bereaved and conducting funerals; running the parish and organizing fund-raising activities.

IN THE GLOSSARY

Anglican Church ✣ Apostle ✣ Baptism
Baptist Church ✣ Bible ✣ Bishop
Celibacy ✣ Church of England
Confirmation ✣ Deacon
Eucharist ✣ Free Church ✣ Holy Spirit
Infant Baptism ✣ Mass
Methodist Church ✣ Minister
Nuptual Mass ✣ Orthodox Church
Protestant Church ✣ Priest
Quakers ✣ Roman Catholic Church
Sacrament

MONKS,
NUNS, AND
PILGRIMS

*"This is the Rule and way of life
of the brothers minor;
to observe the holy Gospel of our
Lord Jesus Christ, living in
obedience, without personal
possessions, and in chastity."*

RULE OF ST FRANCIS

7.1
THE MONASTIC LIFE

Some of the early Christians wanted to give themselves wholly to God. Following Jesus' example, they too went off into desert areas to take up the life of prayer. St. Anthony of Egypt was probably the first but he was soon followed by many others.

There were two reasons why the desert was believed to be a spiritually important location:

a. It allowed people to follow a life of self-denial without any of the normal material comforts.

b. It was believed to be the home of evil spirits; therefore it was an appropriate scene for many conflicts between the powers of good and evil.

In the first few centuries after the birth of the Christian Church, those Christians who retreated from the world tended to live on their own, as hermits. Eventually they began to join together to form religious communities, known as monasteries. One of the earliest was on Mount Athos in Greece, today still inhabited by monks of the Orthodox Church.

LEFT: *In the Middle Ages, before the invention of the printing press, monks made copies of the Bible. The text was often illustrated with paintings, like the one shown here.*

Rule of St Francis 1223

"This is the Rule and way of life of the brothers minor; to observe the holy Gospel of our Lord Jesus Christ, living in obedience, without personal possessions, and in chastity."

Rule of St. Benedict XIVIII [sixth century]

"Idleness is the enemy of the soul. And, therefore, at fixed times, the brothers ought to be occupied in manual labor; and again, at fixed times, in sacred reading."

MONASTIC ORDERS

St. Benedict formed the first monastic Order, which became known as the "Black Monks" because of the color of their habits. By the end of the 13th century there were more than 2,000 religious houses all following the Rule of Benedict. Three important religious Orders had recently come into existence:

a. THE CISTERCIANS. This Order, founded by Bernard of Clervaux in 1098, believed that the Benedictines had become too worldly, and it rebuked popes and emperors alike for the way they lived. Bernard taught his followers the importance of the Virgin Mary to Christian faith; the value of private prayer and meditation, and the importance of making a private rather than a public confession of sins.

b. THE FRANCISCANS. In Italy a nobleman, Francis of Assisi, inspired many people in the 13th century by the way that he imitated the simple lifestyle of Jesus. He gave up all of his possessions and traveled from town to town preaching a message of repentance, trust, and respect for the whole of creation. After spending much time begging, the Order finally turned to the Catholic Church for support.

ABOVE: Modern monks, like those of the Middle Ages, live a life of prayer and study.

✢ ✢ ✢

THE RULE OF ST. BENEDICT

✢ ✢ ✢

St. Benedict [480–547] was the most influential figure in the monastic movement because he laid down a series of rules [called The Rule] for those who joined him in the monastery at Monte Cassino, Italy. The Rule, later adopted by other monastic Orders, stipulated that all monks and nuns should do the following:

a. Live in absolute poverty with no earthly possessions of their own. Property brought with them when they join the Order should be transferred to the monastery or convent.

b. Live in total obedience to the will of the community as it is expressed through its leader. In a monastery this is the Abbot, and in a convent the Mother Superior. These leaders are chosen by the monks and nuns themselves because of the holiness of their lives.

c. Abstain from all sexual contact and intercourse and live in total chastity. Nuns in many Orders wear a gold ring to signify that they are married to God. The Rule emphasizes the close link between community prayer, work, and relaxation in the monastic life. Traditionally, prayers are said seven times a day in monasteries and convents – morning prayers [lauds]; the first hour [prime]; the third hour [terce]; the sixth hour [sext]; the ninth hour [none]; evening prayers [vespers]; and final night prayer [compline]. Modern monastic communities also emphasize prayer, although the number of times for communal prayer has been reduced.

Also in the 13th century an Order of nuns, called the "Poor Clares," was formed and followed the same Franciscan principles.
c. THE DOMINICANS. Founded in 1216 the Dominicans dedicated themselves from the beginning to teaching. As a community the Dominicans broke with tradition by appointing Abbots for a limited time only.

Other religious Orders also developed. The Carmelites and the Augustinians, for instance, placed themselves at the disposal of the Pope, offering preaching and confession to the people and setting up many foreign missions. During the 16th century St. John of the Cross and St. Teresa of Avila set up a reformed Order of Carmelites called the "Discalced" [barefoot]. This Order was intended to follow a stricter regime than the original Order.

IN THE GLOSSARY

Abbot ✢ Convent ✢ Hermit
Meditation ✢ Monastery ✢ Monk
Pope ✢ Roman Catholic Church
Virgin Mary

7.2
TAIZE AND IONA

Although the old monastic traditions and Orders still survive, they have largely failed to capture the hearts and the imaginations of young Christians in modern times. Instead, Christians have turned in large and increasing numbers to such communities as those established at Iona, in Scotland, during the 1930s and at Taize, in France, which grew out of World War II. These two communities embrace many of the old monastic ideals but incorporate modern Christian concerns and ways of worshiping.

THE IONA COMMUNITY

It was in the sixth century that St. Columba used the Scottish island of Iona as a base from which to carry the Christian Gospel to the "pagans" in Scotland and northern England. Much has been written about Columba's attractive personality, his skill as a bard and scribe, his visions and prophecies, and his miraculous powers as he showed when he expelled a water monster from Loch Ness by making the sign of the cross over the water. He built a monastery in Iona although the community eventually died out. Iona, though, remained a holy place in the imagination of many and continued to attract a few pilgrims.

During the 1930s the number of pilgrims increased until, in 1938, the Rev. George Macleod decided to rebuild the monastery using unemployed people from the poor areas of Glasgow. He wanted them to learn about living in a community so that they could return home to improve the quality of their lives. From the beginning Church ministers and working people were attracted to the Iona project since it gave them a wonderful opportunity to talk, pray, and plan before returning to their work physically and spiritually refreshed - and the same thing still happens today on the island.

Gradually the Iona community developed its own distinctive lifestyle. It does not have any monks or nuns but some 250 full members and more than 1,000 associate members. Hundreds of young people also go to summer camps each year to pray, discuss important social issues, work, and make friends. No one lives on the island permanently. Instead they covenant with the community to:

✤ spend one week on the island each year taking part in spiritual and practical activities.

✤ spend some time each day when not in the community reading their Bible and praying.

✤ give 10% of their money [a tithe] to the Church and to work within their own local community for peace, reconciliation, and justice.

RIGHT: The Iona community is unique in character and distinctive in its witness to the Christian Gospel.

✤ look after the welfare of all God's creatures by following a vegetarian lifestyle, eating only eggs from "free-range" chickens, and drinking coffee only from organizations that guarantee that the bulk of the profits go to the coffee growers.

TAIZE

Taize, like Iona, is a religious community that offers spiritual refreshment to people drawn from a wide variety of Christian denominations - including Protestant and Roman Catholic believers. Since 1949 young people have traveled to this location in France to worship with a growing community, which places the theme of reconciliation at the center of its life and worship. When they arrive, visitors find monks of all denominations living and witnessing together to their common faith. This vision was born in

1940 when Roger Schulze bought a house in Taize, France, at the very time when Europe was beginning to feel the ravages of war. Intending to set up a religious community there he began by living the life of a monk alone, praying three times a day and living off the land. Soon he welcomed many refugees to the house who were fleeing from the Nazis in occupied

Part of the Rule of Taize

"That Christ may grow in me, I must know my own weakness and that of my brothers. For them I will become all things to all, and even give my life, for Christ's sake and the Gospel's…"

Europe. However, before long, he was forced to leave France but after the war was over he returned and began to offer food and shelter to German prisoners in a nearby camp. This was unpopular with many of Schulze's neighbors but the theme of Taize, reconciliation, was in place from the beginning.

Today there are over 80 brothers in the community serving God in Taize and at many other centers throughout the world. These brothers see themselves as "Signs of the presence of Christ among men and women and the bearers of God's joy…"

Roger Schulze, or Brother Roger as he is called, is the Abbot of the community. In 1962 a group of German Christians were

moving around Europe building signs of reconciliation in those places that had suffered worst at Nazi hands. They built the Church of Reconciliation at Taize and this is now visited by thousands of travelers, usually young people, each year from all over the world. They are invited to spend a week with the community and to extend their stay, if they wish, with a further week of silence.

IN THE GLOSSARY

Abbot ✤ Bible ✤ Gospel ✤ Iona
Minister ✤ Monastery ✤ Monk
Protestant Church
Roman Catholic Church ✤ Taize
Tithe

7.3
PILGRIMAGES

Although making a pilgrimage is a strong obligation in religions such as Hinduism and Islam this is not the case with Christianity. However, many Christians over the centuries have traveled to "holy places" that are associated with important people or events in Christian history. They have usually traveled on a mission to seek forgiveness or healing. Such pilgrimages have generally been undertaken by Roman Catholic pilgrims, with Protestant believers showing a marked lack of interest in such holy journeys.

CHRISTIAN PILGRIMAGES

Christian pilgrimages do not seem to have started until the fourth century when St. Helena, the mother of the Christian Roman Emperor, Constantine, claimed to have discovered part of the original cross on which Christ had died in Jerusalem. As soon as the news of her discovery spread pilgrims from Europe made their way, in great numbers, to the city. By the

Geoffrey Chaucer.
The Canterbury Tales. Prologue

" Than longen folk to goon
on pilgrimages."

Middle Ages pilgrimages had become a very important part of the Christian faith. Huge numbers of people were making journeys that were fraught with danger to the Holy Land - and many perished there.

There were also many shrines much nearer to home for people throughout Europe. In many places reported visions or miracles drew pilgrims in the thousands. The supernatural manifestations were often associated with a saint who had been buried in a shrine or with some relic brought back from the Holy Land and buried. During the Middle Ages there was a lively trade in such relics although the vast majority of them turned out to be fakes. Some of the holy places achieved lasting recognition such as Walsingham, in Norfolk, England, and Santiago de Compostella, in Spain, while others soon passed into oblivion.

WHY MAKE A PILGRIMAGE?

Pilgrims, then, have been traveling to holy places for centuries. Often these journeys involved great personal hardship. Why, though, have so many people been prepared to put their lives at risk to pray and worship in a shrine far from home? There have been many reasons:

a. THE NEED TO THANK GOD, the Virgin Mary, or some saint for blessings that have been received in answer to a prayer.

b. TO SEEK SOME KIND OF PHYSICAL OR SPIRITUAL BLESSING. Often a shrine is associated with healing - either through the original saint associated with it or through a subsequent appearance of the Virgin Mary at the place. Perhaps the best-known shrine associated with healing is

Maxim Gorky. The Lower Depths

"All of us are pilgrims on this earth.
I have heard it said that the earth itself
is a pilgrim in the heavens."

that at Lourdes, in France, where more than 2,000,000 pilgrims each year go to seek peace and healing. It does not seem to matter that there are few attested healings actually associated with Lourdes - or similar shrines.

c. AS AN ACT OF PENANCE TO SEEK FORGIVENESS FOR SINS. Canterbury Cathedral in England became the leading pilgrimage destination in the Middle Ages after Thomas Becket, the Archbishop of

Canterbury, was murdered on the steps of the altar by knights of King Henry II. The murder had been committed because of angry words spoken by the king. To atone for his sin the king made a pilgrimage to Canterbury in order to seek the forgiveness of God and the Archbishop. A pilgrimage, undertaken with great personal self-sacrifice, was often considered to be the only way to atone for committing such a heinous sin as murder.

d. TO VISIT THE PLACES MOST CLOSELY ASSOCIATED WITH JESUS, Peter, and Paul in the Holy Land. Although many Christians visit places associated with the earthly life of Jesus throughout the year they particularly try to be in those places that are linked with his birth [Bethlehem and Nazareth] and his death [Jerusalem] at

ABOVE: At the end of the 20th century pilgrimages are more popular than they have been for centuries.

John Bunyan. The Pilgrim's Progress

"There's no discouragement
Shall make him once relent
His first avow'd intent
To be a pilgrim."

Christmas and Easter. These pilgrims believe that they will gain a fresh insight into the meaning of the four Gospels and the teachings of Jesus Christ when they travel to these places, although they are also, at the same time, searching for the roots of their faith as well.

To be truthful, many Christian pilgrims return home disappointed. They have sought a blessing or a healing that has not happened. Others return to speak of the experience deepening their own spiritual lives, due to the experience of fellowship and friendship gained through sharing their "spiritual journey" with others.

IN THE GLOSSARY

Altar ✦ Archbishop of Canterbury
Bethlehem ✦ Christmas ✦ Constantine
Easter ✦ Gospels ✦ Holy Land
Jerusalem ✦ Lourdes ✦ Nazareth
Protestant Church ✦ Reformation
Relic ✦ Roman Catholic Church
Saint ✦ Santiago de Compostella ✦ Shrine
Virgin Mary ✦ Walsingham

7.4
HOLY PLACES

There are many Christian "holy places" in Britain and throughout Europe. Except for the Holy Land of Israel, where Jesus lived and died, most of these holy places are associated with either the burial of a saint or a "vision" of the Virgin Mary.

These "holy places" can be divided easily into four categories:

1. THE HOLY PLACES ASSOCIATED WITH THE SAINTS. An old belief that James, one of the original disciples of Jesus, had visited Spain soon after Jesus left the earth seemed to have been confirmed in the ninth century by the discovery of some bones. These were thought to have been those of the Apostle. Unfortunately, in 1589, the Bishop of Compostella, believing that the bones were about to be stolen, hid them - and promptly died without telling anyone where they were! They were not rediscovered until 1879 by which time Santiago de Compostella had become a major pilgrimage destination at the end of the famous "pilgrims" route.

In the 12th century, as we saw in section 7.3, Thomas Becket was murdered on the steps of his altar by four knights loyal to King Henry II. The Archbishop was caught up in a struggle with the king over the power and autonomy of the Church in England. Within three years of his death Becket had been declared a saint by the Church because of the numerous reported miracles at his shrine.

The spot where Becket died became very holy, as did three other locations in the cathedral where parts of his body were buried - the altar and two shrines.

Walter Hilton.
The Scale of Perfection [1494]

"If thou covet to come to this blessed sight of very peace and be a true pilgrim to Jerusalem-ward, though it be so that I were never there, nevertheless as far forth as I can I shall set thee on the way thitherward."

---

2. HOLY PLACES ASSOCIATED WITH THE VIRGIN MARY. We have already mentioned Lourdes, in France, in 7.3. since it was there, in 1858, that a 14-year-old peasant girl, Bernadette Soubirous, claimed to have had a series of visions of the Virgin Mary. A spring of water miraculously appeared and healings have been associated with the shrine since 1873. Since then Lourdes has become the most famous of all Christian shrines attracting no less than 2,000,000 pilgrims every year. The Catholic Church, however, is reluctant to claim that more than a mere handful of miracles have taken place there. A replica of the shrine at Lourdes has been created in the United States.

The similarities are strong between the shrine at Lourdes and that at Walsingham, in Norfolk, England. It was there, in the 11th century, that Lady Richeldis had a vision of the Virgin Mary and was told to build an exact replica of the house of Jesus in Nazareth. A well at Walsingham is credited with having the same healing properties as the one in Lourdes. The Walsingham shrine was destroyed during the Reformation in 1538 but, in 1922, the vicar of Walsingham placed a statue of the Virgin Mary in his church. This became the nucleus of a shrine and, before long, pilgrimages were being arranged to the town. A separate building to house the shrine, known as the Holy House, was erected in 1931 and as the building was extended in 1938 a separate Orthodox chapel was added. The Medieval Slipper shrine was opened as a Roman Catholic chapel in 1934. Special pilgrimages take place to Walsingham each Easter although pilgrims travel to the town throughout the year.

3. PLACES ASSOCIATED WITH JESUS.
The Church of the Nativity in Bethlehem
is built on the supposed site of the stable
in which Jesus was born. Along with other
sites in the Holy Land this one is shared
by the main Christian denominations. The
church has altars that are tended by Greek
Orthodox, Serbian Orthodox, Egyptian
Orthodox, and Roman Catholic priests.
Two other churches in Jerusalem claim to
be standing on the exact location where
the Angel Gabriel appeared to Mary and
announced that she was going to bear
God's Son.

Most Christians, though, visit
Jerusalem to see the places associated with
the death of Jesus. Churches are now

Leo Tolstoy. Master and Men.
'Two Old Men'

"Of what avail is it to go across the sea to
Christ if all the time I lose the Christ that
is within me here?"

standing on the traditional location of
Golgotha, the "place of the skull," where
Jesus was crucified, as well as on the site of
the Garden tomb in which his body was
laid. Many Christian pilgrims also choose
to walk in the footsteps of Jesus up the Via
Dolorosa [the Way of Grief] following the
same path that Jesus took from Pilate's
Judgment-Hall to the place of his
execution. On the way the pilgrims will
pass the 14 Stations of the Cross erected
at those places where Jesus is thought to
have stopped. On Good Friday, many
Christians walk along this route following
behind a wooden cross.

4. PLACES ASSOCIATED WITH THE
APOSTLES AND SAINTS. Each year
thousands of Christian pilgrims travel to
Rome - the "Eternal City" - where St.
Peter is thought to be buried in the
cathedral that bears his name. This spot is
particularly important for Roman
Catholics who believe that their Pope is
the direct successor to the Apostle Peter.
On Easter Sunday the Pope addresses the
many pilgrims that gather in St. Peter's
Square; the Pope speaks to the pilgrims in
their own language.

ABOVE: *Thousands of Christians make a*
pilgrimage every year to holy shrines such as
Lourdes in search of God's blessing.

IN THE GLOSSARY
Altar ✦ Apostle ✦ Archbishop
Bethlehem ✦ Cathedral ✦ Disciple
Easter ✦ Good Friday ✦ Jerusalem
Lourdes ✦ Orthodox Church ✦ Peter
Pilate ✦ Pope ✦ Priest ✦ Reformation
Stations of the Cross
Roman Catholic Church ✦ Saint
Shrine ✦ Walsingham ✦ Virgin Mary

CHRISTIAN BELIEFS

"Love your enemies and pray for those who persecute you, so that you may become the children of your Father in heaven."

MATTHEW 5.48

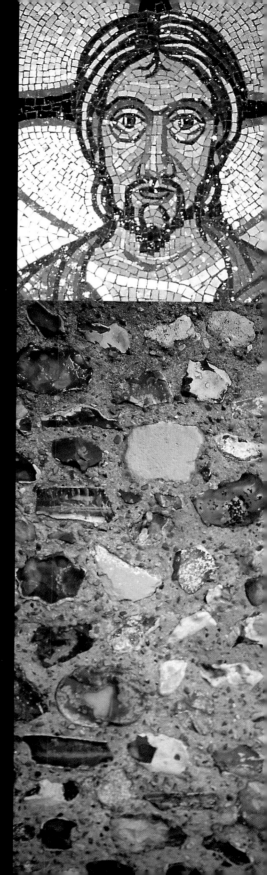

8.1
THE TRINITY

The Christian religion is built upon the fundamental belief that there is one God alone [monotheism] - a belief that it shares with Judaism and Islam, among other religions. Christianity, though, departs from these other faiths in believing that God has revealed himself in three forms - as the Father, Son, and Holy Spirit. The relationship that binds together these three distinct, and yet perfectly united, members of the Godhead is known as the "Trinity." This belief is unique to Christianity and, throughout the ages, Christians have often been misunderstood as believing in three Gods. To Christians, however, belief in "tritheism" [three gods] is heresy.

GOD THE FATHER

From the opening words of the Bible - "In the beginning, when God created the universe..." [Genesis 1.1] - to the very end the Bible insists on certain "truths" about God. Among them are the following:

a. GOD IS THE "GIVER" OF ALL LIFE, THE CREATOR OF EVERYTHING THAT EXISTS. This includes the heavens, the universe, the world, nature, and human beings. Everything owes its initial, and continued, existence to God.

b. GOD IS THE FATHER OF EVERYTHING THAT LIVES. Just as we expect a human father to look after his offspring with devotion and care so God does the same for all he has created. Jesus expressed this graphically when he spoke of God being aware of each sparrow that falls to the ground and numbering the hairs on each human head [Matthew 10.26-31].

c. GOD IS A PERSONAL AND NOT AN ABSTRACT FORCE. He is so deeply involved in the world that he even takes on the sufferings of those he has created.

GOD THE SON

All men and women are sons and daughters of God since, as Genesis says, they are made in God's image. Yet, Jesus is uniquely God's Son. The Incarnation, God taking on human form, is the mystery that stands at the very heart of Christianity. It was as God that Jesus was born into a Jewish family in Palestine, put to death by Pontius Pilate, and brought back to life three days later. At some future time the same Jesus will return to the earth again but this time he will come as its king and judge - an event known to Christian believers as the "Second Coming." History, and the whole of life as we know it, will end when this happens.

Matthew 5.48

"Love your enemies and pray for those who persecute you, so that you may become the children of your Father in heaven."

Philippians 2.5-8

Paul encouraged his readers to follow the Christian life by looking to the example of Jesus:
"He always had the nature of God, but he did not think that by force he should try to remain equal with God. Instead of this, of his own free will he gave up all that he had, and took the nature of a servant. He became like a human being and appeared in human likeness. He was humble and walked the path of obedience all the way to death - his death on the cross."

John 14.16,17

"If you love me, you will obey my commandments. I will ask the Father and he will give you another Helper, who will stay with you for ever. He is the Spirit who reveals the truth about God."

LEFT: *Jesus has been described as "the human face of God." Christians believe that Jesus was the supreme revelation of God.*

GOD THE HOLY SPIRIT

Before he left the earth Jesus promised his followers that the Father would send to them "another helper" and Christians believe that God honored this on the Day of Pentecost when the Holy Spirit became God's power on earth. The same Holy Spirit was also called the "Advocate" who would tell his followers what to say when they were brought before emperors, tribunals, and other courts of law.

TO SUM UP

The Trinity is a revelation more than anything else. God the Father has revealed himself to the world as its creator who sent his Son, Jesus Christ, to save it. Jesus provided the only revelation of God that the human race has received. Without this revelation the world could know nothing about God. The Holy Spirit is God active in today's world.

IN THE GLOSSARY

Bible ✤ Day of Pentecost
✤ Holy Spirit ✤ Incarnation
Trinity

8.2

THE CREEDS

Several Creeds [statements of Christian belief] have been drawn up during the long history of the Christian Church. Only three of them, however - the Apostles' Creed, the Nicene Creed, and the Athanasian Creed - have been widely used in Christian worship.

THE CREEDS

Remnants of the earliest Christian Creeds can be found in the New Testament. These were set formulae of words that were taught to young converts - often as part of their preparation for being baptized. When

The Athanasian Creed

"Whosoever will be saved; before all things it is necessary that he hold the Catholic faith. Which Faith except everyone do keep whole and undefiled; without doubt he shall perish everlastingly."

a person was baptized he or she would then repeat a longer statement of faith, parts of which still survive in some of the letters of Paul. The shortest, and earliest, of these statements of faith is believed to be "Jesus is Lord" [1 Corinthians 12.3] but statements about God the Father and the Holy Spirit were soon added [1 Corinthians 8.6; 1 Timothy 2.5-6].

Three Creeds, in particular, were incorporated into Church worship at a later stage:

✛ ✛ ✛

THE NICENE CREED

✛ ✛ ✛

"We believe in one God…We believe in one Lord, Jesus Christ…God from God, Light from Light, true God from true God… of one being with the Father… For us men and our salvation he came down from heaven; by the power of the Holy Spirit, he became incarnate of the Virgin Mary and was made man. For our sake he was crucified under Pontius Pilate; he suffered death and was buried. On the third day he rose again… He will come again in glory… we believe in the Holy Spirit… we believe in one holy, catholic and apostolic church…"

RIGHT: *The Eastern Orthodox Church, like many of the Western Churches, uses the Christian Creeds in its services.*

Paul and the Creed
[1 Corinthians 15.3, 4]

In one of his statements that was probably repeating an early Christian Creed Paul wrote:

"I passed on to you what I received, which is of the greatest importance: that Christ died for our sins, as written in the Scriptures; that he was buried and that he was raised to life three days later, as written in the Scriptures…"

a. THE NICENE CREED. It was thought that this originated from the Council of the Church called by the Emperor Constantine at Nicea in 325 but this now seems unlikely. All that can be said for certain is that the Nicene Creed was used widely in the Eucharist service by the fifth century. The Orthodox Church uses the Nicene Creed in its Infant Baptism service.

b. THE APOSTLES' CREED. Once thought to date back to the Apostles of Jesus, and the oldest of all Creeds, we now know that it did not exist in its present form until the 11th century. Less complicated than the Nicene Creed, the Apostles' Creed has been suggested as a basis of belief around which all of the major Christian Churches could unite.

c. THE ATHANASIAN CREED. Dates from the fourth or fifth centuries and too long to be used widely in Christian worship.

USING THE CREEDS

While the Creeds are of little interest or importance to Protestants they continue to play an important role in other Churches. During most Anglican, Roman Catholic, and Orthodox services the congregation turn to face the altar before repeating one of the Creeds together. By doing this they are demonstrating their unity together and showing that what unites them is far more important than what separates them. It is strange, though, that there has been little attempt to revise the Creeds even though the way that people think and feel about their Christian faith has changed considerably over the centuries.

All of the Creeds concern themselves with those doctrines, or beliefs, that stand at the heart of the Christian faith:
- the oneness of God.
- the Incarnation of Jesus - the birth of God in human flesh.
- the life, suffering, and death of Jesus.
- the return of Jesus to life after death.
- the return of Jesus to the earth to be its judge.
- the Holy Spirit.
- the "holy, catholic and apostolic" Church.

In theory, the Creeds fulfill the same purpose within the Christian Church as they always have done - to preserve its traditional beliefs and to protect the Church from the teachings of those who have departed from the faith [heretics].

IN THE GLOSSARY

Altar ✤ Anglican Church ✤ Apostle
Apostles' Creed ✤ Athanasian Creed
Creed ✤ Easter ✤ Eucharist
Heretic ✤ Holy Spirit ✤ Incarnation
Infant Baptism ✤ New Testament
Nicene Creed ✤ Orthodox Church
Paul ✤ Protestant Church
Roman Catholic Church

8.3
THE DEATH OF JESUS

The Creeds, which have played a very important role in the Church for centuries, express the Christian commitment to a God who has acted in the world - to create it and to save it. That is why the Creeds are so taken up with Jesus - and, in particular, his death.

Romans 5.6-10

"For when we were still helpless, Christ died for the wicked at the time that God chose... God has shown how much he loved us - it was while we were yet sinners that Christ died for us ... We were God's enemies, but he made us his friends through the death of his Son."

THE DEATH OF JESUS

The crucifixion and resurrection of Jesus are central to any understanding of Christianity. In the Western expression of the faith the sufferings of Jesus on the cross have emphasized the way in which God and human beings have been brought together [reconciled] after sin had separated them. Other pictures taken from the New Testament show us just how this salvation works:

a. JESUS WAS THE INNOCENT LAMB who was sacrificed just as the Jews sacrificed a lamb, without blemish, each year in the Temple to atone, by its blood, for the sins of the whole nation. This blood provided the means by which the holy God could forgive the sins of the people. This was a vivid picture to help Christians understand the death of Jesus, although they believed that Jesus, the perfect Lamb of God, needed only to die once to offer eternal forgiveness.

b. THE DEATH OF JESUS BROUGHT ABOUT THE FINAL DEFEAT OF THE POWERS OF DARKNESS AND EVIL which had always been opposed to God. Earlier in his ministry we are told that Jesus fought against these enemies when he healed the sick and cast

Colossians 2.15

"And on that cross Christ freed himself from the power of the spiritual rulers and authorites; he made a public spectacle of them by leading them as captives in his victory procession."

out demons. His conquering of death, and return to life, was the final defeat for these powers. Through this victory Paul and the early Christians believed that all human beings could be set free from the twin powers of evil and death.

c. BY HIS DEATH JESUS WAS ABLE TO PAY THE PENALTY that God had placed on the

1 Peter. 1.18

" For you know what was paid to set you free from the worthless manner of life handed down by your ancestors. It was not something that can be destroyed, such as silver and gold; it was the costly sacrifice of Christ, who was like a lamb without defect or flaw.

RIGHT: *In the New Testament the death of Jesus is presented as the supreme example of the love that God has for the human race. By his death, Jesus atoned for the sins of the human race.*

human race because of its sinfulness. Being altogether holy by nature, God could only punish sin, and the penalty carried by the human race was too heavy for it to carry. Jesus, though, by his totally unwarranted death was able to pay the penalty and release the human race from its bondage.

PICTURES AND
WAYS OF UNDERSTANDING

These are, of course, only "pictures" that give Christians a way of understanding the death of Jesus. Paul drew most of his

1 John. 4.9,10

"And God showed his love for us by sending his only Son into the world, so that we might have life through him. This is what love is; it is not that we have loved God, but that he loved us and sent his Son to be the means by which our sins are forgiven."

ideas from the imagery and thought of the religion out of which Christianity grew - Judaism. Brought together, these pictures present the death of Jesus Christ as an "atonement," an act that brought together God and human beings. However, for Christians today, the most effective pictures or imagery of the death of Jesus are those that spring out of worship - especially the Holy Communion service. In the Roman Catholic Mass, for instance, the death of Jesus Christ is an eternal act that is "reenacted" each time Christians come together to eat his flesh and drink his blood. In the Protestant form of Holy Communion, however, Christians come together to celebrate as a family the once-and-for-all death of Jesus. However, all Christians would agree with the dominant New Testament picture of the death of Jesus Christ as the supreme example of the love that God has for the whole human race - and the world that he has created.

IN THE GLOSSARY

Creed ✤ Devil ✤ Holy Communion
Mass ✤ New Testament ✤ Paul
Protestant Church ✤ Temple

8.4
THE VIRGIN MARY

It seems likely that Mary was little more than a teenager when she was betrothed to be married to Joseph, a carpenter, from Nazareth. The Gospels tell us that the Angel Gabriel announced to her that she was going to give birth to God's Son, the Messiah [the Annunciation]. Both Matthew and Luke suggest that this birth was brought about by supernatural means without a human father being involved - a belief called the "Virgin Birth."

THE VIRGIN BIRTH

The Nicene Creed makes it clear that the early Church believed that Jesus was "born of a virgin." This simply means that Jesus was conceived in the womb of a virgin, and two of the Gospels explain this mystery by saying that Jesus Christ was conceived by God's Holy Spirit. Strangely, though, this divinely inspired miracle is not mentioned elsewhere in the

Martin Luther, Protestant Reformer

"…the same One who God begot from eternity she herself brought forth in time."

New Testament although a whole succession of Church Councils, from Nicea onward, insisted that Jesus was born to a virgin. From the outset the Christian Church used the virgin birth of Jesus to teach that Jesus is unique, perfect, and divine. If Jesus had been conceived like other human beings he would have shared their sinful nature. He could not then have been able to save the world through his death since that demanded the sacrifice of a blameless life.

BELIEFS ABOUT MARY

The Roman Catholic Church holds three specific beliefs about Mary, the mother of Jesus. It maintains that these beliefs have developed over the centuries under the guidance of the Holy Spirit. Not all of these beliefs are found in the Scriptures but, the Church claims, there is nothing in them that is contrary to the teaching of the Bible. These Roman Catholic beliefs about Mary are as follows:

a. MARY WAS A VIRGIN when Jesus was conceived and born and remained so for the rest of her life [the perpetual virginity of Mary].

b. MARY WAS BORN WITHOUT ORIGINAL SIN so that she might be the perfect recipient for the infant Jesus. This belief, known as the "Immaculate Conception," sets Mary apart from the rest of the human race since

RIGHT: *Both Roman Catholics and Orthodox Christians call Mary "the Mother of God" [Theotokos] because she was the bearer of God's Son.*

The Catechism of the Catholic Church

"The Church… by receiving the word of God in faith becomes herself a mother. By preaching and baptism she brings forth sons and daughters who are conceived by the Holy Spirit and are born to God, to a new and immortal life."

everyone else is born with natural sinful tendencies ["original sin"]. This teaching became part of the official teaching of the Roman Catholic Church in 1854. Pope Pius IX consulted with 603 bishops and only 56 of them opposed the teaching. The Roman Catholic Church celebrates the Feast of the Immaculate Conception on December 8th, while the Orthodox Church, which also shares the belief, celebrates it a day later.

Roman Catholic Prayer

"Alone of all women, Mother and Virgin, Mother most happy, Virgin most pure, now we sinful as we are, we salute thee, we honor thee as how we may with our humble offerings; may the Son grant us that by imitating thy most holy manners, we also, by the grace of the Holy Ghost, may deserve spiritually to conceive the Lord Jesus Christ in our inmost soul, and once conceived never to lose him. Amen."

c. MARY WAS TAKEN UP INTO HEAVEN at the end of her life, body and soul, without dying - the Assumption of the Virgin Mary. Few Popes were more devoted to the Virgin Mary than Pope Pius XII who died in 1958. He was particularly devoted to Our Lady of Fatima who "appeared" to three small children in the Portuguese town of Fatima in 1917. When he dedicated the whole world to the Immaculate Heart of Mary in 1942 he spoke in Portuguese to emphasize his devotion to Fatima.

In 1950, Pope Pius promulgated the doctrine of the Assumption of the Virgin Mary. Roman Catholics share this belief with Orthodox Christians who call this belief the "Dormition." They believe that Mary's "crowning glory…was to be preserved from the corruption of the tomb" and to be lifted, body and soul, into heaven. There Mary reigns as Queen "at the right hand of her Son, the immortal King of Ages." Both Churches celebrate the Feast of the Assumption of Mary on August 15th.

IN THE GLOSSARY

Annunciation ✛ Bible ✛ Bishop
Dormition ✛ Gospels ✛ Holy Spirit
Immaculate Conception ✛ Luke
Matthew ✛ Mary ✛ Messiah
New Testament ✛ Nicene Creed
Orthodox Church ✛ Protestant Church
Virgin Birth

8.5
SUFFERING

Suffering is a universal experience and affects everyone, to a greater or lesser extent, at some time or other. To those who, like Christians, believe in a God who loves and cares for all he has made, this suffering present an enormous challenge to faith. Morever it is not just the "'fact" of suffering that causes such anguish, it is also the "unfairness" of it all. Some people suffer far more than others. Some parts of the world are far more prone to natural disasters than others, while children and adults dying from malnutrition have simply had the misfortune to have been born in the wrong place. Hunger and natural disasters alone are responsible for more than 20 million deaths each year. This causes many problems for the believer in God. All of them, however, boil down to one basic dilemma, which can be put in this way:

EITHER God wants to remove suffering
but cannot – in which case
he is not all-powerful.

✢ ✢ ✢

OR God can remove all suffering
but chooses not to do so –
in which case he is not all-loving.

Job 1.21

After hearing that he had lost everything Job said: *"I was born with nothing and I will die with nothing. The Lord gave and now he has taken away. May his name be praised."*
The author added: *"In spite of everything that had happened, Job did not sin by blaming God."*

CHRISTIANITY AND SUFFERING

Every religion puts forward its own answers to the problem of suffering, and Christianity is no exception. Many of the answers put forward by the Christian faith have been inherited from the much older faith of Judaism. Here are some of the ideas found in the Bible:

a. GOD ALONE KNOWS THE REASON FOR SUFFERING. The classic book on suffering is that of Job and after considering the suffering of one righteous man - Job - the author concludes that suffering is a great mystery and to ask questions about it shows a lack of faith in God. Yet how can anyone witness suffering on any scale and fail to ask the awkward questions?

b. SUFFERING IS THE DIRECT CONSEQUENCE OF SIN. This was the view held by most people in New Testament times and lay behind the encounter between Jesus and the blind man [John 3]. Passing the man his disciples asked Jesus: "Teacher, whose sin caused him to be born blind? Was it his own or his parents' sin?"

The disciples had in mind the statement of God on Mount Sinai that he brought punishment on those who hated him down to the third or fourth generation [Exodus 20.5]. Jesus rejected any idea that the man's blindness might be

Shusaku Endo. Silence

"Something even more sickening, the silence of God. In the face of this terrible sacrifice…Like the sea, God was silent. The silence of God was something I could not fathom."

ABOVE: This 19th-century painting shows Jesus blessing the children. When he was on earth, Jesus showed his love for the innocence of all children.

due to sin - but then enigmatically suggested that his blindness might have been brought about so that "God's power might be seen at work in him" [John 9.3].

c. SIN COMES THROUGH THE ACTIVITY OF SATAN. In the New Testament Satan is the supreme opponent of God with human beings caught up in the eternal battle between good [God] and evil [Satan].

d. SIN AND SUFFERING ARE INEVITABLE IF ALL HUMAN BEINGS ARE TO BE FREE TO CHOOSE THEIR OWN DESTINIES. Some people bring suffering on themselves by making the wrong moral choices.

The answer to human suffering, for the believer in God, must lie with faith. No single answer covers the full extent of suffering, and those who continue to believe in God, despite the unexplained suffering in the world, must have compelling reasons for doing so. Most Christians continue to trust in God as an active power for good, although some, like Dietrich Bonhoeffer, find comfort in the powerlessness of God and his willingness to share in the sufferings of his followers.

Dietrich Bonhoeffer [martyred German Christian leader]. Letters and Papers from Prison

"God is weak and powerless in the world, and that is precisely the way, the only way, in which he is with us and helps us…
Only the suffering God can help."

IN THE GLOSSARY

Bible ✛ Disciples
New Testament ✛ Satan

✤ ✤ ✤ A ✤ ✤ ✤

Abbot: the head of a Benedictine monastery.

Abraham: a Hebrew who lived around 1700 B.C.E., founder of the Jewish nation.

Absolution: forgiveness for wrong-doings, granted by priest.

Acts of the Apostles: fifth book of the New Testament, describes early history of Christian Church.

Advent: from Latin word meaning "arrival," season of preparation for Christmas.

All Saints' Day: day on which Roman Catholics thank God for all holy people.

All Souls' Day: Roman Catholic and Orthodox festival to pray for the souls of those who have died.

Altar: from Latin word meaning "high," table where bread and wine used in Holy Communion are blessed.

Alternative Service Book: the Anglican Prayer Book published in 1980.

Angel: the Greek word for "messenger," used in the Bible for an envoy sent by God.

Anglican Church: worldwide fellowship of Churches based on teachings of Church of England.

Anglo-Catholics: members of the Church of England who adopt many practices of the Roman Catholic Church.

Annunciation: Roman Catholic festival to celebrate appearance of Angel Gabriel to Mary.

Apocrypha: from Greek word meaning "hidden," collection of books included by Roman Catholics and Orthodox believers in their Bible.

Apostle: from Greek verb "to send," applied to disciples of Jesus after Resurrection.

Apostles' Creed: one of the oldest statements of faith in the Christian Church.

Aramaic: the language spoken by everyone in Palestine at the time of Jesus.

Archbishop of Canterbury: the leader of the Anglican Communion.

Ascension Day: day on which some Churches celebrate ascension of Jesus into heaven.

Ash Wednesday: first day of Lent, time for repentance.

Assemblies of God: one of the earliest Pentecostal Churches.

Assumption of Virgin Mary: Roman Catholic and Orthodox festival celebrating translation of Virgin Mary into heaven.

Athanasian Creed: early Christian Creed, not used widely due to length.

Authorized Version: version of Bible authorized by King James I of England, published in 1611.

✤ ✤ ✤ B ✤ ✤ ✤

Baptism: sacrament by which children or adults become members of the Church.

Baptist Church: one of the largest Protestant denominations, open to baptized believers.

Beatitudes: promises made by Jesus in Matthew 5 of blessings for people who showed certain spiritual characteristics.

Believer's Baptism: practice of Baptist Church, and some others, of baptizing only adults who believe in Jesus.

Bethlehem: small town five miles south of Jerusalem, birthplace of King David and Jesus.

Bible: the sacred book of the Christian Church.

Bishop: office of leadership in the Anglican/Episcopal, Roman Catholic, and Orthodox Churches, traced back to New Testament.

Bishop of Rome: title given to Pope, Peter believed to be first holder of title.

Blasphemy: any form of words or actions that shows contempt for God.

Book of Common Prayer: authorized prayer book of Anglican Church, drawn up during Reformation by Archbishop Thomas Cranmer.

Breaking of Bread: favorite Protestant term for Holy Communion.

✤ ✤ ✤ C ✤ ✤ ✤

Caiaphas: the Jewish High Priest at the time of Jesus.

Calvary: hill just outside city of Jerusalem where Jesus was crucified.

Canon: the "rule" that decided which books to include in the Bible.

Cathedral: the main church in the diocese, where bishop has his seat i.e. cathedra.

Celibacy: demand that Roman Catholic priests live without any sexual relationships.

Charismatic Movement: interdenominational movement that places emphasis on the gifts of the Spirit.

Chrism: oil used in church services such as Confirmation and Ordination.

Chrismation: service in Orthodox Church that follows Baptism.

Christ: means "the Anointed One," Greek form of Hebrew word "Messiah."

Christmas: Christian festival to celebrate birth of Jesus.

Church of England: Church formed after King Henry VIII fell out with the Pope over his divorce, made Established Church in England by Queen Elizabeth I.

Confirmation: service in Anglican and Roman Catholic Churches, bishop lays his hands on the head of each person.

Constantine: [274-337], the first Christian Roman Emperor who established Christianity as first religion of State.

Convent: house in which nuns live.

Citadel: place of worship for members of the Salvation Army.

Contemplation: an advanced form of praying.

Council of Jerusalem: Council held in Jerusalem in 51 C.E. of church leaders, to decide basis on which Gentiles to be admitted into Church.

Creed: a statement of Christian belief.

Crucifix: cross carrying figure of Jesus, found in church and worn around the neck.

✤ ✤ ✤ D ✤ ✤ ✤

Day of Pentecost: day on which the Holy Spirit was given to the early Christians.

David: ideal Jewish king, ancestor of Jesus.

Deacon: one of three "holy orders" in Roman Catholic, Orthodox, and Anglican Churches, the others being that of bishop and priest.

Devil: the supreme force of evil, the one opposed to God and Jesus.

Disciple: "pupil," follower of Jesus.

Divine Liturgy: the equivalent of the Eucharist in the Orthodox Church.

✤ ✤ ✤ E ✤ ✤ ✤

Easter: festival at which Christians remember the death and resurrection of Jesus.

Elim Church: early Church within the Pentecostal Movement.

Epiphany: festival after Christmas to celebrate visit of Wise Men to Jesus.

Episcopacy: the system of Church government that includes bishops.

Episcopalian Church: independent Church in the United States, member of the Anglican Communion.

Epistle: a letter, written by one of the Apostles in the New Testament.

Eucharist: "thanksgiving," sharing bread and wine in memory of the death of Jesus (in Anglican Church).

Evangelical: member of any Protestant denomination who believes in the divine inspiration of the Bible and personal conversion to Christ.

Excommunication: ultimate punishment imposed by the Roman Catholic Church, bars person from receiving any of the sacraments of the Church.

Exodus: journey of Israelites out of Egyptian slavery, second book in Bible.

Exorcism: practice of casting a demon out of a person.

Extreme Unction: anointing with oil of sick person in Roman Catholic Church.

✤ ✤ ✤ F ✤ ✤ ✤

Feast of Weeks: see Pentecost.

Font: stone or wooden receptacle to hold water for Infant Baptism.

Free Churches: Nonconformist Churches, Churches free of links with Church of England.

✤ ✤ ✤ G ✤ ✤ ✤

Gethsemane: garden in Jerusalem where Jesus prayed before crucifixion.

Gloria Patri: important Roman Catholic prayer.

Golgotha: "place of skull," place where Jesus was crucified.

Good Friday: the day on which Christians remember the death of Jesus.

Good News Version: modern translation of the Bible, first published in 1966.

Gospel: message of "Good News" preached by early Christians.

Gospels: the four books at start of New Testament, contain the story of Jesus.

✤ ✤ ✤ H ✤ ✤ ✤

Hail Mary: important Roman Catholic prayer to Virgin Mary.

Heaven: the home of God and his angels.

Hell: the place of everlasting torment and punishment, reserved for those who have lived their lives without faith in God.

Heretic: a person whose teaching is disowned by the Church.

Hermit: a man or a woman who lives a totally solitary existence.

Herod the Great: [70-4 B.C.E.], Jewish king who ruled Judea for Romans, king at time of birth of Jesus.

High Church: Anglican Churches that are close to being Roman Catholic.

High Priest: leader of the Jews at time of Jesus.

Holy Communion: the meal of bread and wine shared by Christians to commemorate the death of Jesus.

Holy Orders: three vocations within the Roman Catholic, Anglican/Episcopal and Orthodox Churches, bishop, priest and deacon.

Holy Saturday: the Saturday of Holy Week, recalling time when Jesus was buried.

Holy Spirit: part of the Christian Trinity, the power of God in the world.

Holy Week: the week in the Church year running through from Palm Sunday to Easter Sunday.

Host: The wafer used in the Roman Catholic Mass.

House-Church Movement: groups of Christians who worship in houses rather than in church.

✢ ✢ ✢ I ✢ ✢ ✢

Icon: a special painting used by Orthodox Christians to help them to pray.

Iconostasis: screen in front of altar in Orthodox church, covered with icons.

Incarnation: God becoming flesh, applied to Jesus who was born to Mary and Joseph.

Indulgence: an act of merit undertaken by someone to lessen the time someone else spends in purgatory.

Infant Baptism: practice of many Churches of baptizing babies.

Intercessions: prayers said on behalf of someone else.

Iona: old religious community off Scotland.

✢ ✢ ✢ J ✢ ✢ ✢

James: brother of John, disciple of Jesus, leader of church in Jerusalem.

Jerusalem: city captured by King David, home to Temple built by King Solomon and rebuilt by Herod the Great.

Jerusalem Bible: Roman Catholic version of Bible published in 1966.

John: son of Zebedee, one of disciples of Jesus, author of one Gospel, several epistles, and the book of Revelation.

John the Baptist: cousin of Jesus, sent by God to prepare way for coming of Messiah.

Joseph: father of Jesus.

Judas Iscariot: disciple of Jesus, one who betrayed him to the Jewish leaders.

✢ ✢ ✢ K ✢ ✢ ✢

Kingdom of God: the rule of God in the hearts of people, brought in by Jesus.

✢ ✢ ✢ L ✢ ✢ ✢

Last Supper: the last meal that Jesus enjoyed with his disciples.

Lectern: desk from which the Bible lesson is read at front of church.

Lectionary: a system followed by many Churches to ensure that the Bible is read systematically in public.

Lent: season of preparation in many Churches for Easter.

Liturgy: worship of a Church, set down in its prayer book.

Lord's Prayer: prayer taught by Jesus to his disciples, used in almost all services.

Lord's Supper: favorite Protestant description for service of Holy Communion.

Lourdes: Roman Catholic shrine in France, visited by millions of pilgrims.

Low Church: Church of England churches that are Protestant and Evangelical.

Luke: doctor and companion of Paul on travels, author of third Gospel.

Lutheran Church: Protestant Church based on teachings of Martin Luther, the Reformer.

✢ ✢ ✢ M ✢ ✢ ✢

Magisterium: the teaching of the Roman Catholic Church, comes from the Pope and the bishops when they meet together in Council.

Mark: accompanied Paul and Barnabas on first missionary journey, writer of second Gospel.

Martyr: a person who dies for their faith.

Mary: mother of Jesus.

Mass: the Roman Catholic name for the Eucharist.

Matthew: tax-gatherer, disciple of Jesus, author of first Gospel.

Maundy Thursday: day on which Christians remember Jesus washing the feet of his disciples.

Meditation: a form of mental prayer.

Messiah: Hebrew form of Greek word meaning "the Anointed One," deliverer promised by God to the Jews.

Methodist Church: important Protestant Church in England and the United States, based on teachings of John Wesley.

Minister: person who leads the preaching and teaching in a Protestant church.
Mishnah: the Jewish oral law.
Missal: the Roman Catholic Prayer Book.
Monastery: house in which monks live.
Monk: member of Religious Order who accepts three vows of chastity, obedience, and poverty.
Moses: leader and law-giver in ancient Israel, led Israelites out of Egyptian slavery.

✤ ✤ ✤ N ✤ ✤ ✤

Nave: passageway down the center of a church with pews on either side.
Nazareth: village in Galilee in which Jesus spent his childhood and early manhood.
New Testament: the second part of the Bible, contains the Gospels and the letters written by the Apostles.
Nicene Creed: the statement of belief thought to have come from the Nicene Council called by Constantine in 325.
Nonconformist Church: a Protestant Church that was born because its members could not "conform" to the teaching of the Church of England.
Nuptial Mass: Mass celebrated at the end of a wedding in a Roman Catholic church.

✤ ✤ ✤ O ✤ ✤ ✤

Old Testament: the Christian title for the books of the Jewish Scriptures.
Ordination: services that admits person to "holy orders" and makes him a priest.
Orthodox Church: family of Churches found mainly in Eastern Europe and the Middle East.
Our Father: name for the Lord's Prayer in Roman Catholic Church.

✤ ✤ ✤ P ✤ ✤ ✤

Palestine: originally "Canaan," area that was homeland to Jews, called Israel in 1948.
Palm Sunday: festival day on which Christians celebrate the triumphal entry of Jesus into Jerusalem.
Paschal Candle: the candle lit in many churches on Holy Saturday, used for 40 days after Easter.
Passover: Jewish festival to celebrate release of Israelites from Egyptian slavery, also called Pesach.
Parable: a human story carrying a spiritual or moral message.
Pater Noster: Latin title for the Lord's Prayer.
Patriarch: the senior bishop in one of the Orthodox Churches.
Paul: persecutor of Christians, converted on Damascus Road, leader of early Church, missionary, letter-writer, and church planter.
Peace: the Peace is exchanged during Holy Communion in many Churches.
Penance: a penalty imposed by a priest because of a sin admitted in confession.
Pentecost: Greek name for the Festival of Weeks.
Peter: most prominent disciple of Jesus, early leader of Church.
Pharisees: "the separated ones," most influential Jewish group at time of Jesus.
Pontius Pilate: Roman procurator of Judea between 26 and 36 C.E., signed death-warrant of Jesus.
Pope: title given to Bishop of Rome, the successor of St. Peter and leader of world's Roman Catholics.
Presbyterian Church: a Church based on leadership by presbyters [elders].

Priest: person authorized to lead worship in Orthodox, Anglican/Episcopalian, and Roman Catholic Churches.
Prophet: man sent by God to proclaim his message.
Psalm: a Jewish holy song, collected into Old Testament book of Psalms.
Pulpit: raised platform in church from which sermon is given.
Purgatory: place in which, according to Roman Catholics, people spend a time of preparation before heaven.

✤ ✤ ✤ Q ✤ ✤ ✤

Quakers: Christian denomination started in 17th century by George Fox, favors extensive use of silence in services.

✤ ✤ ✤ R ✤ ✤ ✤

Rabbi: a leader of the Jewish community.
Reformation: 16th-century movement in Europe, broke the power of the Roman Catholic Church by insisting that salvation came through faith and not works.
Relic: remains of saint or some clothing associated with them, treated with great reverence in Roman Catholic and Orthodox Churches.
Requiem Mass: special Mass said at Roman Catholic funeral.
Reserved Sacrament: the practice of keeping consecrated bread [rarely wine] for use at later Mass.
Roman Catholic Church: community of Christians throughout world that follows leadership of the Pope as St. Peter's successor on earth.
Rood-screen: screen across Anglican Churches to separate altar from the people.

Royal Doors: the doors in the iconostasis in Orthodox church, opened to allow priest through during Divine Liturgy.

✢ ✢ ✢ S ✢ ✢ ✢

Sabbath Day: the seventh day of the Jewish week, set apart by God's command for rest and worship.

Saint: a person who is exceptionally holy and leads a life of devotion to God.

Salvation Army: Protestant organization founded by William Booth in 1878.

Sacrament: an external, physical sign of an inward, spiritual blessing.

Sanhedrin: highest Jewish Court, met in Jerusalem with 71 members.

Santiago de Compostella: holy place in Spain, associated with death of James.

Satan: superhuman being in the Bible who is the main enemy of God and the leader of all the rebellious angels.

Scribe: Jewish interpreter and teacher of the law of Moses in time of Jesus.

Septuagint: the Greek version of the Hebrew Bible, translated in the third century B.C.E.

Sermon: part of service in which minister or priest explains a passage from the Bible.

Sermon on the Mount: the title given to the teachings of Jesus collected together by Matthew in chapters 5 to 7 of his Gospel.

Shavuot: Feast of Weeks.

Shrine: a building containing the bones of a saint or holy person.

Shrove Tuesday: day on which confessions were heard and absolution given, day before Lent started.

Society of Friends: the Quakers.

Son of God: a title given in the Bible to the Messiah.

Son of Man: Jesus' favorite description of himself, stressed his oneness with the human race.

Speaking in Tongues: practice in Pentecostal and Charismatic Churches of speaking and praying in unknown languages.

Stations of the Cross: 14 carvings or paintings around Catholic church, telling story of death of Jesus.

Stephen: first Christian martyr, whose death was described in Acts of the Apostles.

Sunday: "the day of the sun," first day of the week replacing the Jewish Sabbath Day in Christian worship.

Synagogue: Jewish place of worship.

Synoptic Gospels: "looking together"; first three Gospels, which take a similar approach to the life of Jesus.

✢ ✢ ✢ T ✢ ✢ ✢

Tabernacle: small cupboard behind altar in Roman Catholic church holding the Reserved Sacrament.

Taize: community of monks founded in France in 1944.

Temple: center of pilgrimage for all Jews in Jerusalem, especially during the three great festivals.

Ten Commandments: laws given by God to Moses on Mount Sinai.

Thirty-Nine Articles: statement of beliefs held by the Church of England dating from the 16th century.

Tithe: practice in Old Testament of giving one-tenth of all produce and income each year to God.

Torah: teaching, God's Law found in first five books of Old Testament.

Transubstantiation: Roman Catholic teaching that, during the Mass, the bread and wine turn into the actual body and blood of Christ.

Trinity: central teaching of the Christian faith that there are three persons in one God - God the Father, God the Son, and God the Holy Spirit.

✢ ✢ ✢ U ✢ ✢ ✢

United Reformed Church: Church formed from amalgamation of Congregational and Presbyterian Churches in 1972.

✢ ✢ ✢ V ✢ ✢ ✢

Viaticum: Holy Communion given in the Catholic Church to someone who is dying.

Virgin Birth: teaching that Mary conceived Jesus by the Holy Spirit without having had sexual intercourse.

Votive Candle: a candle lit in a Roman Catholic church to accompany a prayer.

Vulgate: the Latin translation of the Bible widely used between the 5th and 16th centuries.

✢ ✢ ✢ W ✢ ✢ ✢

Walsingham: the most important place of Christian pilgrimage in Britain.

Whitsun: another name for Pentecost, celebrates the coming of the Holy Spirit to the disciples in Jerusalem.